THE

FOUNDERS OF MARYLAND.

THE

FOUNDERS OF MARYLAND

AS PORTRAYED IN

MANUSCRIPTS, PROVINCIAL RECORDS AND EARLY DOCUMENTS,

BY

REV. EDWARD D. NEILL, A. B.,

AUTHOR OF "ENGLISH COLONIZATION OF AMERICA," "VIRGINIA COMPANY OF LONDON," "TERRA MARIÆ," "FAIRFAXES OF ENGLAND AND AMERICA," "HISTORY OF MINNESOTA," ETC.

"Nec falsa dicere, nec vera reticere."

ALBANY:
JOEL MUNSELL.
1876.

PREFACE.

Every year, the citizens of ancient Padua crowd the costly church, dedicated to their townsman, the Italian Saint Anthony, and hang upon its walls, or around the shrine, sketches in oil, or water colors, commemorative of important events in their lives.

One of the many good results of the centennial year of the American Republic, is the taking down from the garrets, the neglected portraits of our forefathers, the removal of the stains and dust, the substitution of new frames, for those battered and worm eaten, and in remembering their labors for posterity.

With the aid of manuscripts, brought to light during the last decade, and access to the papers of the British Record Office, we can now portray more accurately, and hang in a better light, the FOUNDERS OF MARYLAND.

The object of this little book, is to state facts, which had become obscured or forgotten, concerning the first European settlers on the shores of the Potomac River, and Chesapeake Bay.

Bearing in mind, the sentiment of Hieronymus in a letter to Epiphanius: "Malem aliena verecunde dicere, quam jura imprudenter ingerere," I have recorded facts, gleaned from the manuscript Provincial Records at the capital of Maryland, and other documents of the Provincial period, rather than obtruded my own opinions.

EDWARD D. NEILL.

Macalester College,
near Falls of Saint Anthony,
Minnesota.

CONTENTS.

FOUNDERS OF MARYLAND.

HENRY FLEET.

BEFORE the charter of Maryland was granted, English men, engaged in the beaver trade, had settled upon the isles and shores of the Chesapeake Bay and its tributaries. As one turns over the pages of the large manuscript volumes in folio, prepared by the Secretary of the London Company, he reads that on July 21st, 1621, a paper was read from Ensign Savage, relating to the great trade of furs, by Frenchmen, in the Great Bay. The letters of John Pory, Secretary of the Virginia Colony, also informed the Company of a discovery, by him and others, into the Great Bay northward, where he left "settled, very happily, near an hundred Englishmen, with hope of a good trade of furs." Among the first points, occupied by traders, was the island situated at the head of the Chesapeake Bay, near the mouth of the Susquehanna River, which was called Palmer's Island, after Edward Palmer, a nephew of the unfortunate Sir Thomas Overbury, poisoned by the malicious arrangements of the wanton wife of the Earl of Somerset. Camden speaks of Palmer as a curious and diligent antiquary, and the quaint Fuller writes:

"His plenteous estate afforded him opportunity to put forward the ingenuity implanted by nature, for the public good, resolving to erect an academy in Virginia. In order whereunto he purchased an island, called Palmer's Island unto this day, but in pursuance thereof was at many thousand pounds expense, some instruments employed therein, not discharging the trust reposed in them with corresponding fidelity."[1]

Another point, occupied by the whites was the junction of Potomac Creek with Potomac River, in what is now Strafford County, Virginia. In the fall of 1621 the ship Warwick and pinnace Tiger, sailed from the Thames with supplies, and thirty-eight young women, selected with care, as wives for Virginia planters. On the voyage, the Captain of the Tiger fell in with a vessel of Turks, and was captured, but at length, was rescued by the coming up of another friendly ship, in company of which, he arrived with the maids, at Jamestown. The Tiger was then sent under Spilman, an experienced trader, with twenty-six men to trade for corn in the upper Potomac, and they

---

[1] Palmer's Island, as marked upon Augustine Hermann's Map of Virginia and Maryland, published in 1673, which I have examined in the British Museum, is the island now known as Watson's Island, a few rods above the bridge of the Philadelphia, Wilmington and Baltimore Railway.

erected a stockade at Potomac Creek. On this voyage, with twenty-one men, Spilman landed among the Anacostans, who lived on and near the site of the city of Washington, and five men remained on board, who were attacked by the savages, whom they repulsed, by the discharge of cannon. Those on shore were either killed or made prisoners, and among the latter was Henry Fleet, who became one of the prominent associates of Governor Calvert, in establishing the Province of Maryland.

After a capitivity of several years he returned to England, and magnified the truth in the manner of Hennepin and La Hontan. One of the letter writers of that day says: "Here is one, whose name is Fleet, newly come from Virginia, who being lately ransomed from the Indians, with whom he hath long lived, till he hath left his own language, reporteth that he hath oftentimes been within sight of the South Seas, that he hath seen Indians besprinkle their paintings with powder of gold, that he had likewise seen rare precious stones among them, and plenty of black fox, which of all others is the richest fur."[1]

By his rose-colored representations, he induced London merchants, to engage in the Potomac beaver trade. In September, 1627, William Cloberry a prominent London merchant, placed the Paramour, a vessel of

---

[1] Mead, in Streeter's Early Maryland Papers.

one hundred tons, in charge of Fleet.[1] Four years later, Fleet is again in England, and on the 4th day of July, 1631, the ship Warwick with John Dunton as Master, and Henry Fleet factor, sailed for America. After visiting New England, the vessel, on the 21st of October, arrived at the mouth of James River, in Chesapeake Bay. Five days later, he reached the town of Yowaccomoco, where he had lived with the Indians for several years, and found that they, by reason of his absence, had burned the beaver skins, as was their custom. He then entered into an agreement that they should preserve the furs during the winter, and promised that he would come in the spring, and give them merchandize in exchange. Receiving eight hundred bushels of Indian corn, he sailed on the 6th of December, but owing to a storm, was obliged to anchor in James River. Fleet writes to his partners in London: "Divers that seemed to be my friends, advised me to visit the Governor.[2] I showed myself

[1] Bruce's British State Papers.

[2] Governor John Harvey was, in early life, a captain in the East Indies. Late in the year 1629, he succeeded Pott, as Governor of Virginia. On the 15th of September 1634 Lord Baltimore asked Windebank, Secretary of State, to thank Harvey for assistance rendered the Maryland Colony. Three days after the King's Secretary sent a flattering note to the Governor. On the 16th of December Harvey wrote "Desirous to do Lord Baltimore all the service he is able, but his power is not great, being limited by his commission, to the greater number of voices at the Council table, where almost all are against him, especially when it concerns Maryland."

In May 1635 he was deposed as Governor and sent to England by

willing, yet watched an opportunity that might be convenient for my purpose, being not minded to adventure my fortunes at the disposing of the Governor." On the 10th of January he slipped away from Point Comfort, and on the 7th of February, was trading with the fishermen of the New England coast. On the 6th of March, he stopped at the Isle of Shoals, near Portsmouth, New Hampshire, and procured provisions, for a return voyage, and from thence, went to Massachusetts Bay.

On the 9th of April, 1632, in company with a pinnace of twenty tons, Fleet steered for Southern waters. On the 13th of May, he arrived at the Accomac settlement, of which Captain William Clayborne was the prominent man. After a visit of three days, Clayborne in a small vessel accompanied him across the Chesapeake Bay. Eight days after this, he arrived again at Yowaccomoco, and found that one Charles Harman [1]

---

the Council, for the usurpation of power without respect to the vote of the Council, and for upholding the Marylanders in attacking Clayborne's pinnace, and for knocking out some of the teeth of a Capt. Stevens with a cudgel.

The King on the 2d of April 1636 gave Harvey a new commission as Governor, and on the 18th of January 1637 returned to Jamestown and resumed his position. He was succeeded by Sir Francis Wyatt in November 1639, and died after much bodily suffering, leaving many debts.

[1] Charles Harman was a planter of Accomac and at this time thirty-two years of age. He came to Virginia in 1622, in the Ship Furtherance. In 1625 his servants on his plantation were John Askume aged twenty-two, and Robert Fennell who came in 1624 in the ship Charles,

an Indian trader had already secured most of the beaver. Resting here, he immediately sent his brother Edward toward the Falls of the Potomac, to secure furs. On the 26th of May, he reached the town of Potomac, in what is now Strafford County, Va., and on the 1st of June, sent back the pinnace of twenty tons, with a cargo of Indian corn, and proceeded to Piscattoway the residence of a powerful chief, and from thence, visited the Anacostans, an adjoining band, who traded with the Canada Indians, and by whom he had been captured several years before. On Tuesday, the 26th of June, he anchored two leagues below the Falls of the Potomac, in the vicinity of what is now the city of Washington. He writes, in his journal, which is still preserved, in the library of Lambeth Palace:

"This place without all question is the most pleasant and healthful place in all this country, and most convenient for habitation, the air temperate in summer, and not violent in winter. The 27th of June, I manned my shallop, and went up with the flood, the tide rising four feet, at this place. We had not rowed above three miles, but we might hear the Falls to roar, about six miles distant."

After trading with the Indians in the neighborhood, he returned to Piscattoway, about fifteen miles below

and James Knott aged twenty-three who came in 1617 in the ship George. Harman at one time represented Accomac in the Virginia Assembly.

Washington, and on the 28th of August, met a boat, containing John Utie a Virginia councillor, Charles Harmon a trader, and six others who came to bring him before Governor Harvey for illicit trading.

The Governor was grasping and unscrupulous and seems to have winked at Fleet's irregularities. On the 7th of September, the latter anchored at Jamestown, and writes in his journal: "The Governor, bearing himself like a noble gentleman, showed me very much favor, and used me with unexpected courtesy. Captain Utie did acquaint the Council with the success of the voyage, and every man seemed to be desirous to be a partner with me. * * * * * The Court was called the 14th of September, where an order was made, which I have here enclosed, and I find that the Governor hath favored me therein."

There is in the Public Record Office, at London, a complaint of Griffith & Co., owners of the ship Warwick, in which they state that three years before, they had sent the ship to Virginia, for trade and discovery, of which Henry Fleet was factor, with commission to return in a year, but, that by authority of Governor Harvey, Fleet had retained the vessel and its profits to their great loss.[1]

Other London merchants in that day found the Virginians slippery fellows, and were ready to endorse

---

[1] Sainsbury's State Papers.

the sentiments of the Dutch captain De Vries, who had been a guest of Governor Harvey, and wrote as follows in his book of voyages: "The English there are very hospitable, but they are not proper persons to trade with. You must look out when you trade with them, Peter is always by Paul or you will be stuck in the tail. If they can deceive any one, they account it among themselves a Roman action. They say in their language, 'He played him an English trick.'"

The next mention of Fleet, is in connection with th settlement of the Calvert colony. Governor Leonard Calvert, before landing his company made a reconnoissance of the Potomac, as far as Piscattoway. The interpreter, Father White says, was Henry Fleet, and "one of the Protestants of Virginia." The journal of the Jesuit continued: "The Governor had taken with him, as a companion on his voyage, Henry Fleet, a Captain from the Virginia colony, a man especially acceptable to the savages, well versed in their language, and acquainted with the country. This man was at first, very intimate with us, afterwards, being misled by the evil counsels of one Clayborne, he became very hostile to us, and excited the natives to anger against us, by all the means in his power.

"In the meantime, however, while he was still on friendly terms with us, he pointed out to the Governor, a spot so charming in its situation, that Europe can scarcely show one to surpass it." Thus Fleet's old trading post, Yowaccomoco, was transformed into the town of Saint Mary, and Leonard Calvert and his associates began there to build a rival commonwealth to Virginia.

A few weeks after the Calvert colonists landed, on May 9, 1634, there were assigned to Fleet, two thousand acres on St. George River, St. George's Hundred, which was subsequently known as the Manor of West Saint Mary.

In the legislature of 1638, the first Assembly in Maryland, whose records have been preserved, were Henry Fleet and his brothers Edward, John, and Reynold, and on the 21st of the next February another legislature was called by the Governor, to assemble "at the house, where Captain Fleets lately dwelt."

After the civil war in England began, Fleet identified himself with Virginia, and by its legislature on April 5th, 1645, Captain Fleet was authorized "as a fit person acquainted with the language of the Indians, and accustomed to intercourse with them, to trade with the Rappahannocks, or any Indians, not in amity with Opechancanough." The next year, he was appointed to organize an expedition against the Indians, and build a fort, in the valley of the Rappahannoc river. In December, 1652, he sat as a member of the Virginia legislature, from Lancaster County, and with his old rival William Clayborne was authorized "to discover and enjoy such benefits and trades, for fourteen years, as they shall find out in places where no English have ever been and discovered, nor have had particular trade, and to take up such lands, by patents, proving their rights, as they shall think good."

In 1654, he is last mentioned, as an interpreter to a proposed expedition against the Indians. Upon the Coast Survey Map of the Potomac, in the Report of 1860, Fleet's Point appears between the 37th and 38th degrees of latitude, and here perhaps, the old and hardy pioneer may have last lived.

A BRIEF JOURNAL

OF A VOYAGE MADE IN THE BARK VIRGINIA, TO VIRGINIA AND OTHER PARTS OF THE CONTINENT OF AMERICA.

IN the library of the Archbishop of Canterbury, a Lambeth, is a manuscript journal with the above title, writen by Capt. Henry Fleet. In 1664 it belonged to William Griffith A.M., who was, probably, the son of Henry Griffith, one of the owners of the Warwick, and may have been the Oxford graduate, who was Chancellor of dioceses of St. Asaph and Bangor. In presenting the journal to American readers, bad and obsolete spellings have been corrected, with the exception of those of proper names.

JOURNAL.

"The 4th of July 1631, we weighed anchor from the Downs, and sailed for New England, where we arrived in the harbor of Pascattouaie, the 9th of September, making some stay upon the coast of New England. From thence, on Monday the 19th of September, we sailed directly for Virginia, where we came to anchor in the bay there, the 21st of October, but made little stay. From thence we set sail for the river of Potomack, where we arrived the 26th of October at an Indian town called Yowaccomoco, being at the mouth of the river, where I found that, by reason of my absence, the Indians had not preserved their beaver, but burned it, as the custom is, whereupon I endeavoured by persuasion to alter that custom, and to preserve it for me against the next spring, promising to come there with commodities in exchange by the first of April. Here I was tempted to run up the river to the heads, there to trade with a strange populous nation, called Mowhaks,[1] man-eaters, but after good deliberation, I conceived many inconveniences that might fall out. First, I considered that I was engaged to pay a quantity of Indian corn in New England, the neglect whereof might be prejudicial both to them that should have it, and to me that promised payment. And when I observed that winter was very forward, and that if I should proceed and be frozen in, it might be a great hindrance to my proceedings; therefore I did forbear, and making all the convenient haste I could, I took into the barque her lading of Indian corn as I supposed, being persuaded and overruled by John Dunton, whom I entertained as master. But upon the delivery of our lading found not above 800 bushels to our great hindrance.

"The 6th of December we weighed anchor, shaping our course directly for New England, but the wind

[1] The Maquas, Mawhawks, Mowhaks, or Mohawks were then a fierce tribe west and south of Albany, N. Y., but Fleet exaggerates in calling them, man-eaters.

being contrary, ending with a fearful storm, we were forced into the inhabited river of James Town. There were divers envious people, who would have executed their malice upon us had it not been for a rumour of a commission they supposed I had, which I took great pains to procure, but (time being precious and my charge great) I came away only with the copy. Divers that seemed to be my friends advised me to visit the Governor. I showed myself willing, yet watched an opportunity that might be convenient for my purpose, being not minded to adventure my fortunes at the disposing of the Governor.

"Then we did a little replenish our provisions. But at this time I was much troubled with the seamen, all of them resolving not to stir until the spring, alleging that it was impossible to gain a passage in winter, and that the load being corn, was the more dangerous. But the master and his mate, who were engaged for the delivery of the corn, laboured to persuade and encourage them to proceed, showing that it would be for their benefit; so that, with threats and fair persuasions, at last I prevailed.

"On Tuesday, the 10th of January, we set sail from Point Comfort and arrived at Pascattoway, in New England, on Tuesday the 7th of February, where we delivered our corn, the quantity being 700 bushels.

"On Tuesday, the 16th of March, we weighed anchor and sailed to the Isle of Shoals, where we furnished ourselves with provisions of victual. Sunday, the 11th of March, we sailed for the Massachusetts Bay, and arrived there on the 19th day. I wanted commodities to trade with the Indians, and here I endeavoured to fit myself if I could. I did obtain some, but it proved of little value, and was the overthrow of my voyage.

"From the Massachusetts, was sent with me a small pinnace of the burthen of twenty tons, the which I was to freight with Indian corn for trucking stuff, which proved to me like that I had before from the Bay, and Pascattoway, from whence I had some likewise. Yet this was not the greatest wrong I received by this barque, as shall hereafter be related.

"On Monday, the 9th of April, 1632, we both weighed anchor, and shaped our course for Virginia, but the sixth day being stormy weather we lost our pinnace. Contrary winds and gusty weather, with the insufficiency of the master, made our return to Virginia tedious, to the overthrow of the voyage. But it so pleased God that we anchored against the English colony the 13th of May, when, for want of wind, being a flat calm, we came to an anchor at Acomack. Having some English commodities I sold them for tobacco. Wednesday, the 16th of May, we shaped our course for the river of Patomack, with the company of Captain Claybourne, being in a small vessel. By the relation of him and others of the plantation of Acomack, the Governor of Virginia was much displeased with me, unto whom complaints had been made by divers of the country, and it had been discovered by one of my company that was run away, how that I had but the copy of my commission. Friday, the 17th of May, we might discern a sail making toward us about two o'clock in the afternoon. She came up to us, and we found that it was the pinnace that came out with us, which having had a short passage, had been up the river of Patomack, at Yowocomaco, an Indian town, where she had stayed three weeks, and then I was certified, that he who had usually been in those parts with me, after my last departure, came there and went up the river to truck, where he found good store of beaver, and being furnished with commodities such as Virginia affords, did beat about from town to town for beaver, but prevailed not. And in the end, coming where my barque had been, that town having 300 weight of beaver, he then reported that I was dead, they supposing his vessel to be the same that I was to come in, desired them to bring me dead or alive, and this report caused some distraction for the present, who supposed that by reason of my long absence, past my appointed time, some mischance had befallen me. And the Indians there disposed of their beaver to Charles Harman, being 300 weight, who departed but three days before I came there.

"This relation did much trouble me, fearing (having

contrary winds) that the Indians might be persuaded to dispose of all their beaver before they could have notice of my being in safety, they themselves having no use at all for it, being not accustomed to take pains to dress it and make coats of it. Monday, the 21st of May, we came to an anchor at the mouth of the river, where hastening ashore, I sent two Indians, in company with my brother Edward, to the Emperor, being three days' journey towards the Falls. And so sailing to the other side of the river, I sent two Indians more, giving express order to all of them not to miss an Indian town and to certify them of my arrival. But it so happened that he (Harman) had cleared both sides of the river, so far as the Emperor's where these Indians, when they came, certified him of my being well, and of my brother's being there, so that afterwards he could not get a skin, but he made a very hand of it, and an unexpected trade for the time, at a small charge, having gotten 1500 weight of beaver, and cleared fourteen towns. There were yet three that were at the disposing of the Emperor, so the barque and myself passing by divers towns, came to the town of Patomack on Saturday, the 26th of May.[1] There I gave the pinnace her lading of Indian corn, and sent her away the 1st of June, with letters from our company to their friends in London, and elsewhere in England, which were safely conveyed from New England. The

[1] Potomac town supposed to be at the mouth of Potomac Creek in Virginia.

same day, with a north-west wind (Charles Harman staying no longer), we set sail, and the third we arrived at the Emperor's, but before we could come to the town he was paddled aboard, by a petty king, in a canoe.

When he came he used divers speeches, and alleged many circumstances for the excuse of the beaver which Charles Harman had of his men in that river, and after compliments used, he presented me with one hundred and fourteen beaver skins, which put me into a little comfort after so much ill success. Yet this was nothing, in regard to the great change at his town, and at a little town by him called the Nacostines, where I had almost 800 weight of beaver. There is but little friendship between the Emperor, and the Nacostines,[1] he being fearful to punish them, because they are protected by the Massomacks or Cannyda Indians, who have used to convey all such English truck as cometh into the river to the Massomacks.

"The Nacostines before, here occasioned the killing of twenty men of our English, myself then being taken prisoner and detained five years, which was in the time of Sir Francis Wyatt, he being the Governor of Virginia.[2] The 13th of June I had some conference with an interpreter of Massomack[3] and of divers other

[1] The Nacostines or Anacostans lived near the site of the city of Washington. The suburb opposite the Navy Yard is now called Anacostia, and Mason's Island is often called Analostan.

[2] See page 11.

[3] Daniel Gookin, formerly of Virginia and a friend of the Massachusetts Indian missionary, John Eliot, in a History of the Indians in New

Indians that had been lately with them, whose relation was very strange in regard of the abundance of people there, compared to all the other poor number of natives which are in Patomack and places adjacent, where are not above five thousand persons, and also of the infinite store of beaver they use in coats. Divers were the imaginations that I did conceive about this discovery, and understanding that the river was not for shipping, where the people were, not yet for boats to pass, but for canoes only. I found all my neighbor Indians to be against my design, the Pascattowies having had a great slaughter formerly by them to the number of one thousand persons in my time. They coming in their birchen canoes did seek to withdraw me from having any commerce with the other Indians, and the Nacostines were earnest in the matter, because they knew that our trade might hinder their benefit. Yet I endeavored to prosecute my trade with them nevertheless, and therefore made choice of two trusty Indians to be sent along with my brother, who could travel well.

England, writes: "There is a numerous race of Indians that live upon a great lake or sea. Some report it to be salt water, while others fresh. * * * * This people I conceive to be the same that Capt. Smith in his History of Virginia doth in several places call Massawomeks. * * * Now the place where he met with and heard of this great people of Massawomeks was at the head of the Chesapeake Bay or Gulf, which lieth in the latitude of 40 degrees, nearest; and he saith, they had recourse thither from the lakes or seas where they lived, in canoes of bark of trees."

"I find the Indians of that populous place are governed by four kings, whose towns are of several names, Tonhoga,[1] Mosticum, Shaunetowa,[2] and Usserahak,[3] reported above thirty thousand persons, and that they have palisades about the towns made with great trees, and with scaffolds upon the walls. Unto these four kings, I sent four presents in beads, bells, hatchets, knives, and coats, to the value of £8 sterling.

"The 14th of June they set forth, and I entreated them to bring these Indians down to the water to the Falls, where they should find me with the ship. On Monday, the 25th of June, we set sail for the town of Tohoga, when we came to an anchor two leagues short of the Falls,[4] being in the latitude of 41, on the 26th of June. This place without all question is the most pleasant and healthful place in all this country, and most convenient for habitation, the air temperate in summer and not violent in winter. It aboundeth with all manner of fish. The Indians in one night commonly will catch thirty sturgeons in a place where the river is not above twelve fathom broad. And as for deer, buffaloes, bears, turkeys, the woods do swarm with them, and the soil is exceedingly fertile, but above this place the country is rocky and mountainous like Cannida.

[1] Tohogas or Tiogas?

[2] Shawnees?

[3] Outouacs or Ottowas?

[4] Nine miles above Washington.

"The 27th of June I manned my shallop, and went up with the flood, the tide rising about four feet in height at this place. We had not rowed above three miles, but we might hear the Falls to roar about six miles distant, by which it appears that the river is separated with rocks, but only in that one place, for beyond is a fair river. The 3d of July, my brother, with the two Indians, came thither, in which journey they were seven days going, and five days coming back to this place. They all did affirm that in one palisado, and that being the last of thirty, there were three hundred houses, and in every house forty skins at least, in bundles and piles. To this king was delivered the four presents, who dispersed them to the rest. The entertainment they had I omit as tedious to relate. There came with them, one-half of the way, one hundred and ten Indians, laden with beaver, which could not be less than 4000 weight. These Indians were made choice of by the whole nation, to see what we were, what was our intent, and whether friends or foes, and what commodities we had, but they were met with by the way by the Nacostines, who told them we purposed to destroy those that came in our way, in revenge of the Pascattowaies, being hired to do so for 114 skins, which were delivered aforesaid, for a present, as a preparative.

"But see the inventions of devils; the life of my brother, by this tale of the Nacostines, was much endangered. The next morning I went to the Nacostines to know the reason of this business, who answered, they did know no otherwise, but that if I would make a firm league with them, and give their king a a present, then they would undertake to bring those other Indians down. The refusal of this offer, was the greatest folly that I have ever committed, in mine opinion.

"The 10th of July, about one o'clock we discerned an Indian on the other side of the river, who with a shrill sound, cried, 'Quo! Quo! Quo!' holding up a beaver skin upon a pole. I went ashore to him, who then gave me the beaver skin, with his hatchet, and laid down his head with a strange kind of behavior, using some few words, which I learned, but to me it was a foreign language. I cheered him, told him he was a good man, and clapped him on the breast with my hands. Whereupon he started up, and used some complimental speech, leaving his things with me ran up the hill.

"Within the space of half an hour, he returned, with five more, one being a woman, and an interpreter, at which I rejoiced, and so I expressed myself to them, showing them courtesies. These were laden with beaver, and came from a town called Usserahak, where were seven thousand Indians. I carried these Indians aboard, and traded with them for their skins. They drew a plot of their country, and told me there came with them sixty canoes, but were interrupted by the Nacostines, who always do wait for them, and were hindered by them. Yet these, it would seem, were resolute, not fearing death, and would adventure to come down. These promised, if I would show them my truck, to get great store of canoes to come down with one thousand Indians that should trade with me. I had but little, not worth above one hundred pound sterling, and such as was not fit for these Indians to trade with, who delight in hatchets, and knives of large size, broad-cloth, and coats, shirts, and Scottish stockings. The women desire bells, and some kind of beads.

"The 11th of July there came from another place seven lusty men, with strange attire; they had red fringe, and two of them had beaver coats, which they gave me. Their language was haughty, and they seemed to ask me what I did there, and demanded to see my truck, which, upon view, they scorned. They had two axes, such as Captain Kirk traded in Cannida, which he bought at Whits of Wapping, and there I bought mine, and think I had as good as he. But these Indians, after they came aboard, seemed to be fair conditioned, and one of them, taking a piece of chalk, made a plain demonstration of their country, which was nothing different from the former plot drawn by the other Indians. These called themselves Mostikums, but afterwards I found they were of a people three days' journey from these, and were called Hereckeenes,[1] who, with their own beaver, and what they get of those that do adjoin upon them, do drive a trade in Cannida, at the plantation, which is fifteen days' journey from this place. These people delight not in toys, but in useful commodities.

" There was one William Elderton very desirous to go with them, but being cannibals I advised him rather to go with the others, whither I had sent a present, telling him they had no good intentions, yet upon his earnest entreaty, though unwilling, I licensed him to proceed, and sent a present with him to their king, one of them affirming that they were a people of one of the four aforenamed nations. But I advised my man to carry no truck along, lest it might be a means to endanger his life. Nevertheless, as I was afterwards informed, he carried a coat, and other things to the value of ten shillings more, and on the 14th of July departed.

" The 15th of July the Indians were returned with the interpreter, according to promise, and, being come, looked about for William our interpreter, to whom I made relation whither he was gone, and they seemed to lament for him, as if he were lost, saying, that the men with whom he went would eat him, that these people were not their friends, but that they were Herecheenes. At the departure of these Indians, they told

[1] Iroquois?

me that two hundred Indians were come to the place from whence they came with store of English truck to trade for beaver, and told us they had a purpose to come down and visit us, and take a view of our commodities, and they inquired after divers kinds of commodities, of which I had some very good, part of which I gave them, and sent them away, desiring them to follow after the other Indians, and to get away my man. All this time did my truck spend not so much upon beaver as upon victuals, having nothing but what we bought of the Indians, of whom we had fish, beans, and boiled corn. The seamen, nevertheless, hoped to sell away all their clothes for beaver.

"The 18th of July I went to the Pascattowaies, and there excused myself for trading with those that were enemies, and from thence I hired sixteen Indians, and brought them to the ship, and made one of them my merchant, and delivered to them, equally divided, the best part of my truck, which they carried up for me, to trade with their countrymen; and I gave charge to the factor to find out my man, and to bring him along with them when they came back.

"The 7th of August these Indians returned, and the Tohogaes sent me eighty skins with the truck again, who showed these Indians great packs of beaver, saying there were nine hundred of them coming down by winter, after they had received assurance of our love by the Usserahaks, although the Nacostines had much labored the contrary. And yet they were all at a stand for a time, by reason of two rumors that had raised, the one, that I had no good truck, neither for quantity, nor for quality; the other that one of our men was slain by the Hirechenes, three days' journey beyond them, and that they had beguiled us with the name of Mosticums, one of their confederate nations. Nevertheless, they being desirous to have some trial of us, had sent us these skins, minding to have an answer whether we would be so satisfied of this deceit or no, and that they would come all four nations and trade with us upon their guard.

"I liked this motion very well, but was unwilling to protract time, because I had but little victuals, and small store of trucking stuff, and therefore I sailed down to Pascattowie, and so to a town on this side of it called Moyumpse. Here came three cannibals of Usserahak, Tohoga, and Mosticum; these used many complimenting speeches and rude orations, showing that they desired us to stay fifteen days, and they would come with a great number of people that should trade with us as formerly they had spoken. I gave them all courteous entertainment, and so sent them back again.

"At this time I had certain news of a small pinnace with eight men, that made inquiry in all places for me, with whom was Charles Harman.[1] The Indians would

[1] See page 13.

willingly have put them by from me, or I could have shifted them in the night, or taken them, as I pleased; but, knowing my designs to be fair and honest, I feared nothing that might happen by this means. And now, after much toil and some misery, I was desirous of variety of company.

"The 28th of August, in the morning, I discerned the barque, and having the shallop which I built amongst the Indians, I manned her with ten men and all manner of munition, with a full resolution to (discover) what they were, and what were their intentions. Being come near them, I judged what they were and went aboard, where I found Captain John Uty, one of the Council of Virginia.[1] In which barque I stayed with them by the space of two hours, and then invited them aboard my ship, where, being entered into my cabin, after a civil pause, this salutation was used:—

"Captain Fleet, I am sorry to bring ill news, and to trouble you in these courses, being so good; but as I am an instrument, so I pray you to excuse me, for, in the King's name I arrest you, your ship, and goods, and likewise your company, to answer such things as the Governor and Council shall object."

I obeyed; yet I conceived that I might use my own discretion, and most of his company being servants, and ill-used, were willing to have followed me, yea, though it had been to have gone for England.

[1] See notice of Utie on page 48.

"The 29th of August we came to Patomack; here was I tempted to take in corn, and then to proceed for New England; but wanting truck, and having much tobacco due to me in Virginia, I was unwilling to take any irregular course, especially in that I conceived all my hopes and future fortunes depended upon the trade and traffic that was to be had out of this river.

"I took in some provisions, and came down to a town called Patobanos,[1] where I found that all the Indians below the cannibals, which are in number five thousand persons in the river of Patomack, will take pains this winter in the killing of beavers and preserve the furs for me now that they begin to find what benefit may accrue to them thereby. By this means I shall have in readiness at least five or six thousand weight against my next coming to trade there. Thursday, the 6th of September 1632, we came to the river of James Town, and on the 7th day anchored at James Town, and I went ashore the same night.

"The Governor, bearing himself like a noble gentleman, showed me very much favor, and used me with unexpected courtesy. Captain Utye did acquaint the Council with the success of the voyage, and every man seemed to be desirous to be a partner with me in these employments. I made as fair weather as might be with them, to the end I might know what would be

[1] Also called Potopaco and Potobatto, now Port Tobacco.

the business in question and what they would or could object, that I might see what issue it would come to.

"The Court was called the 14th of September, where an order was made, which I have here enclosed, and I find that the Governor hath favored me therein. After this day, I had free power to dispose of myself. Whereupon I took into consideration my business, and what course would be most for mine advantage, and what was fittest for me to resolve upon. I conceived it would be prejudicial to my designs to lose the advantage of the spring, because of the infancy of this project, considering how needful it was to settle this course of trade with the Indians so newly begun, and now that I had gotten £200 worth of (beaver) in readiness, and some of it very good.

"And I having now built a new barque of sixteen tons, and fitted myself with a partner that joineth with me for a moiety in that vessel, which we have sent to the Cannadies with provisions, and such merchandize, are there good commodities, and so to the Medeiras and Tenariffe. The loading is corn, meal, beef, pork, and clapboards. For myself, I hope to be gone up the river within the six days.

"And so, beloved friends, that shall have the perusal of this journal, I hope that you will hold me excused in the method of this relation, and bear with my weakness in penning the same. And consider that time would not permit me to use any rhetoric in the form of this discourse, which, to say truly, I am but a stranger unto as yet, considering that in my infancy and prime time of youth, which might have advantaged my study that way, and enabled me with more learning, I was for many years together compelled to live amongst these people, whose prisoner I was, and by that means am a better proficient in the Indian language than mine own, and am made more able that way.

"The thing that I have endeavored herein is, in plain phrase, to make such relation of my voyage as may give some satisfaction to my good friends, whose longing thoughts may hereby have a little content, by perusing this discourse, wherein it will appear how I proceeded, and what success I have had, and how I am like to speed if God permit. All which particulars, the whole ship's company are ready to testify on behalf of this Journal."

WILLIAM CLAYBORNE.

In the Relation of the Successful Beginnings of Lord Baltimore's Plantation in Maryland, written a few weeks after the landing of Leonard Calvert and associates, it is stated, that William Clayborne came "from parts in Virginia where we intend to plant," and said that the Indians were alarmed, by reason of a rumor that some one had raised, of six ships that were come, with a power of Spaniards."

Clayborne was above the majority of the Virginia colonists in birth and intellectual culture. He had a very different training from Henry Fleet, his rival in the Indian trade, who once wrote "that in my infancy and prime time of youth, I was for years together compelled to live among these people whose prisoner I was, and by that means am a better proficient in the Indian language, than mine own."

He was the second son of Sir Edward Cleburne or Clayborne of Westmoreland, and was one of the colonial officers appointed in 1621, by the London Company for Virginia,and for many years Secretary of the Colony.

Among his early companions at Jamestown were

the estimable Governor, Sir Francis Wyatt and his gentle wife, the niece of Sir Edwin Sandys, the head of the London Company. The chaplain was Rev. Haut Wyatt, A.M., the Governor's brother. The Treasurer of the Colony was George Sandys, poet and translator of Ovid, and brother of Sir Edwin. The Secretary was another poet, Christopher Davison, the son of that Sir William, in whose employ William Brewster of Plymouth Rock once was. The surgeon general John Pott, was also a Master of Arts.[1] In 1621 the London Company writes: "It is our express will that the tenants belonging to every office, be fixed to his certain place, on the lands set out, for which Mr. Cleyburne[2] is chosen to be our Surveyor, who at the Company's very great charge is set out."

In 1627 Clayborne commanded an expedition against the Indians, and landing at the junction of the York and Pamunkey River destroyed the village and corn-

[1] Oxford University in 1605 conferred the degree of A.M. on John Pott and George Calvert afterwards the first Lord Baltimore. See *Wood's Athenæ Oxonienses.*

[2] The name is variously spelt, Cleyburne, Cleburne, Clybourne, Clibourne. The following pedigree is found in the *Visitation of Cumberland,* published by the Harleian Society of London.

Robert Clyborne of Westmoreland.
Edward Clyborne his son.
Children of Edward.
Richard Cliburne.
John Clibourne.
Thomas Clibourne.
William Clibourne.
Elizabeth married John Thwaits.

fields, and for his services received the land on which the Indians had dwelt. In October of this year, one arrived at Jamestown, who caused much dissension.

Lord Baltimore in early life was known as George Calvert, the son of a worthy Yorkshire farmer. A graduate of Oxford, and an attaché of Cecil, Earl of Salisbury, he attracted the attention of James the First, and when about twenty-five years of age, was appointed one of the Secretaries of State.

A good linguist, a ready writer, and possessing executive talent, he was soon recognized as a right hand man of the King, and an antagonist of the people's party in the House of Commons. In 1624 he represented Oxford in Parliament, opposed freedom of speech, and defended the royal prerogative. In 1625 he announced his conversion to the Church of Rome,[1] and when Charles the First came to the throne, the oath of allegiance being offered to him, as one of the Privy Council, he hesitated and was relieved of duties at Court, and went to his estate in Ireland.

While a member of the Church of England, in 1620, he had planted a colony at Ferryland in New Found-

[1] Goodman formerly Bishop of Gloucester of the Church of England, after he united with the Church of Rome, says that Calvert was converted by Gondomar, the Spanish Ambassador, "and Count Arundel whose daughter Secretary Calvert's son had married." This is a strange error. Ann Arundel wife of Cecil Calvert died July 24, 1649, at the age of thirty-four. When Gondomar was in England she was about six years of age, and certainly not married to Secretary Calvert's son.

land, and on May 21st, 1627, he writes to his intimate friend Sir Thomas Wentworth:

"I am heartily sorry, that I am farther from my hopes of seeing you, before my leaving this town, which will be now within these three or four days, being bound for a long journey, to a place which I have had a long desire to visit, and have now the opportunity and leave to do it.

"It is New Foundland I mean, which it imports me more than in curiosity, only to see, for I must either go and settle it in better order or else give it over, and lose all the charges I have been at hitherto, for other men to build their fortunes upon. And I had rather be esteemed a fool by some, for the hazard of one month's journey, than to prove myself one certainly for six years by past, if the business be now lost for the want of a little pains and care."[1]

Arriving at Ferryland on the 23d of July bringing two priests of the Church of Rome, he astonished the minister of the Church of England in charge of the colonists. After a brief visit, he went back to England and in the summer of 1628 returned with a second wife,[2] and several children by his first wife, and a

[1] *Strafford's Letters*, vol. 1, p. 39, Dublin, 1740.

[2] There has been much confusion as to Lord Baltimore's family relations.

Davis and Hildreth erroneously intimate that Governor Leonard Calvert was an illegitimate child, and bore the baton in his escutcheon. Governor Stuyvesant of New York, who corresponded with Governor

Roman Catholic priest. The Church of England clergyman was sent home, and in October complained to the authorities of England, that contrary to law, mass was publicly celebrated in New Foundland. In a few months Lord Baltimore found the country too cold for a residence, and he wrote a letter dated August 19th, 1629, to his old friend King Charles, in which he uses these words.

"Have met with grave difficulties and incumbrances here, which in this place are no longer to be resisted, but enforce me presently to quit my residence and to shift to some other warmer climate of this new world where the winter be shorter and less rigorous.

"For here your Majesty may please to understand that I have found by too dear bought experience, which other men for their private interests always concealed from me, that from the middlest of October, to the middlest of May there is a sad fare of winter upon all this land, both sea and land so frozen for the greater part of the time, as they are not penetrable; no plant or vegetable thing appearing out of the earth until it be about the beginning of May, nor fish in the sea;

Philip Calvert, does however state that Philip was the illegitimate child of Leonard Calvert's father, the first Lord Baltimore.

Lodge, Burke and other writers on the peerage never allude to the second wife of Lord Baltimore. It is possible that he was privately married in Ireland, and not according to the laws of the Church of England. There is a mystery about the second wife. In one of the Ayscough MSS. of the British Museum it is stated that she was lost at sea, and there the subject is dropped.

besides the air is so intolerable cold as it is hardly to be endured.

"By means whereof, and of much salt meat, my house hath been an hospital, all this winter, of 100 persons, fifty sick at a time, myself being one, and nine or ten of them died.

"Hereupon I have had strong temptations to leave all proceedings in plantations, and being much decayed in my strength to retire myself to my former quiet, but my inclination carrying me naturally to these kind of works, and not knowing how better to employ the poor remainder of my days, than with other good subjects, to further the best I may, the enlarging your Majesty's empire in this part of the world, I am determined to commit this place to fishermen that are able to encounter storms and hard weather, and to remove myself with some forty persons to your Majesty's domain, Virginia, where if your Majesty will please to grant me a precinct of land with such privileges as the King, your father was pleased to grant me here, I shall endeavor to the utmost to deserve it." [1]

Waiting for no reply he sailed away, and early in October 1629, with his children and their step-mother and attendants arrived at Jamestown. He expressed a desire to John Pott the acting Governor, who probably received the degree of A.M. from Oxford on

[1] Virginia State Papers.

the same day as he obtained the honor, to settle in that country, but was informed that it was the law that every new-comer should take the oath of allegiance and supremacy, but this he refused and the following statement signed by Governor John Pott, Samuel Matthews, Roger Smyth and William Clayborne prepared on November 30th, 1629, was forwarded to the King's Privy Council.[1]

"May it please your Lordships to understand, that about the beginning of October last, there arrived in the colony the Lord Baltimore, from his plantation at New Foundland, with an intention, as we are informed, rather to plant himself to the southward of the settlement here, although he hath seemed well affected to this place, and willing to make his residence therein with his whole family.

"We were readily inclined to render to his Lordship all those respects which were due unto the honor of his person, which might testify with how much gladness we desire to receive and to entertain him, as being of that eminence and degree whose presence and affection might give great advancement to the plantation.

"Thereupon, according to the instructions from your Lordships, and the usual course held in this place, we tendered the oaths of supremacy and allegiance to

---

[1] Va. MSS. Library of Congress.

his Lordship and some of his followers, who, making profession of the Romish religion, utterly refused to take the same, a thing we could not have doubted in him, whose former employments under his late Majesty might have endeared to us a persuasion he would not have made a denial of that, in point whereof, consists the loyalty and fidelity which every true subject oweth unto his Sovereign.

"His Lordship, therefore, offered to take the oath, a copy whereof is included, but, in true discharge of the trust imposed on us by his Majesty, we could not imagine that so much latitude was left for us to decline from the prescribed form so strictly exacted, and so well justified and defended by the pen of our late Sovereign, King James of happy memory; and among the blessings and favors for which we are bound to bless God, and which this colony hath received from his Most Gracious Majesty, there is none whereby it hath been made more happy than in the freedom of our religion which we have enjoyed, and that no Papists have been suffered to settle their abode amongst us, the continuance whereof we now humbly implore from his Most Sacred Majesty, and earnestly beseech your Lordships, that by your mediations and counsels, the same may be established and confirmed unto us."

Not discouraged by his cold reception, leaving his family, he went to England to sue for a grant of land.

In the British State Paper Office there is the following petition preserved, addressed to Lord Dorchester, Secretary of State, in Baltimore's own hand.

"That your Lordship would be pleased to procure me a letter from my Lords of the Council to the Governor of Virginia in favor of my wife now there, that he would afford her his best assistance upon her return into England in all things reasonable for her accommodation, in her passage and for recovery of any debts due unto me in Virginia, or for disposing of her servants according to the custom of the country if she shall think fit to leave any behind her or upon any other occasion, wherein she may have use of his lawful favor.

"Moreover that your Lordship would be pleased to move his Majesty that whereas upon my humble suit unto him from Newfoundland for a proportion to be granted unto me in Virginia, he was graciously pleased to signify by Sir Francis Cottington that I should have any part not already granted, that his Majesty would give me leave to choose such a part now, and to pass it unto me, with the like power and privileges as the King his father of happy memory did grant me that precinct in Newfoundland, and I shall contribute my best endeavors, with the rest of his loyal subjects, to enlarge his Empire in that part of the world, by such gentlemen and others, as will adventure to join with me, though I go not myself in person."

Joseph Mead, Chaplain of Archbishop Laud, on February 12, 1629–30, writes: "Though his Lordship [Baltimore] is extolling that country to the skies, yet he is preparing a bark to send to fetch his Lady and servants from thence, because the King will not permit him to go back again."

In October, 1629, Sir Robert Heath, the Attorney General of England, obtained a grant of land in America, between the degrees of 31 and 36 of north latitude, under the name of the "Province of Carolana," and two days before Mead wrote, an association of gentlemen asked for two degrees of land, to be held under Heath, as Lord Paramount, with liberty to appoint all officers both civil and ecclesiastical. On April 30, 1630, the Privy Council ordered, that no aliens should be settled in Carolana, without special direction, nor any but Protestants.[1]

Lord Baltimore at length, in February, 1631, secured a tract of land south of James River, and a charter was prepared; but Clayborne, Secretary of Virginia, and ex-Governor Francis West, a brother of late Lord Delaware, then in London, made such representations that it was revoked. Undaunted, he persevered, and on the ground that it was not occupied by English subjects, obtained a grant for lands, north and east of the Potomac.[2] The King said, "Let us name it after

[1] Sainsbury's State Papers.

[2] See Charter.

the Queen. What think you of Mariana?" Baltimore objected, because, that was also the name of the Spanish historian, who taught that the will of the people was higher than the law of tyrants. Charles then modified the name and said, "Let it be Terra Mariæ."[1] At this time, Clayborne had a plantation on the east side of the Chesapeake Bay, and trading posts at Kent Island and Palmer's Island at the mouth of the Susquehanna, the latter of which he claims to have discovered.[2]

As soon as it was known that Lord Baltimore had obtained a patent for the Chesapeake region, on the ground that it had not been occupied, the London partners of Clayborne and Virginia planters complained, that the grant was within their limits, covering the places of their traffic, and so near to their habitations, as will give a general disheartening to the planters if they be divided into several governments. George Lord Baltimore died on April 9, 1632, and his son Cecil succeeded to the title. On the 28th of June, 1633, both parties were heard, and on the 3d of July the Privy Council "for the preventing of further questions and differences did order that the planters on each side shall have free traffic and commerce, each with the other," also that Lord Baltimore should be left to his patent, and the others to the course of law according to their desire.

Upon the arrival of Leonard Calvert's expedition at

[1] Ayscough MSS.
[2] Annapolis MSS.

the James River, Calvert claimed that Clayborne and the people of Kent Island should acknowledge his jurisdiction. As the inhabitants had been represented in the Virginia Legislature, Clayborne consulted the Council of Virginia as to the proper course to pursue, and they replied " that they knew no reason why they should render up the right of the Isle of Kent, more than any other formerly given by his Majesty's patent." Governor Calvert forbade his trading in the Chesapeake without his license, and under the influence of Fleet was made to believe that he was inciting the Indians to resistance.

Clayborne on the 20th of June 1634, held a conference with the Chief of the Patuxents in the presence of George Calvert the brother of the Governor, Frederick the brother of Sir John Winter[1] and others of the Maryland Colony, and two prominent Virginians John Utie[2] and Samuel Mathews.[3] After examining the Chief, through a sworn interpreter, the whole was written out and approved by both Marylanders and Virginians.

[1] Frederick Winter died before 1638; George Calvert lived and died in Virginia.

[2] John Utye or Utie came to Virginia in 1620 in the ship Francis Bona Ventura and was followed in 1621, in the ship Sea Flower by Ann his wife, and an infant son.

[3] Samuel Matthews came to Virginia in 1622, in the ship Southampton, and lived at Blunt Point, a little distance above Newports News. He was thrifty and intelligent. His wife was the daughter of Sir Thomas Hinton. He was a type of the early planter, " lived bravely, kept a good house, and was a true lover of Virginia."

The Chief, in his statement, denied that Clayborne had prejudiced his tribe against the Marylanders, and said that Fleet "was a liar and that if he were present he would tell him so to his face."[1]

The explorer of the Delaware River Captain Thomas Young, a friend of Lord Baltimore, who was at Jamestown in July, 1634, wrote for Secretary Windebank an entirely different version and adds: "This, so far as I can learn, is the true state, wherein my Lord of Baltimore's Plantation stands with those of Virginia, which perhaps may prove dangerous enough for them, if there be not some present order taken in England for suppressing the insolence of Clayborne and his accomplices, and for disjointing this faction, which is so fast linked and united, as I am persuaded will not by the Governor be easily dissevered or overruled, without some strong and powerful addition to his present authority, by some new powers from England. And it will be to little purpose, for my Lord to proceed in his Colony, against which they have so exasperated and incensed all the English Colony of Virginia; as here it is accounted a crime almost as heinous as treason to favor, nay, to speak well of that colony of my Lord's.

"And I have observed myself a palpable kind of strangeness and distance between those of the best sort in the country which have formerly been very

[1] Streeter's Early Papers.

familiar and loving to one another, only because the one hath been suspected to have been a well wisher to the Plantation of Maryland."[1]

Of the Council of Virginia but two were friendly to the Maryland Colony. Lord Baltimore upon receiving intelligence of the position of affairs on the 4th of September, instructed Leonard Calvert and his Commissioners in Maryland, that if Clayborne would not acknowledge his patent, to seize and detain him close prisoner at Saint Mary, and if they can, "take possession of his plantation on the Isle of Kent."

On October 8th however, the King wrote from Hampton Court, to the Virginia Council and all Lieutenants of Provinces in America, requiring "them to be assisting the planters in Ketish Island, that they may peaceably enjoy the fruits of their labors, and forbids Lord Baltimore or his agents to do them any violence."

It is not strange that orders so contradictory should have induced bloodshed. In the spring of 1635, Cornwallis proceeded, as one of the Maryland Commissioners, to search in the waters of the Chesapeake, for Virginians trading without a Maryland license.

The goods of a trader named Harmon were seized, and a pinnace called the Long Tail belonging to Clayborne captured.[2] Clayborne sent from Kent Island a

---

[1] Young in Aspinwall Papers. Mass. Hist. Soc. Publications, 4th Series, vol. ix.

[2] Report of Parliament Committee of the Navy Dec. 31, 1652.

boat with Lt. Ratcliff Warren and thirteen others to recover his property, and on the 23d of April, in the Pocomoke met Commissioner Cornwallis with two pinnaces the St. Margaret and St. Helen, when a conflict took place and William Ashmore of the Maryland side, and Lt. Warren, John Bellson, and William Dawson of the Virginians were killed. Again on the 10th of May, in the harbor of Great Wighcomoco, Cornwallis met Thomas Smith of Kent Island who was arrested, tried for piracy by the Maryland Assembly, and sentenced to be hung.

When the Virginians learned that their Governor, John Harvey, approved of Governor Calvert's course towards Clayborne, they were very indignant, and determined no longer to acknowledge his authority.

Four days after Warren was killed, a public meeting was held at Yorktown at the house of William Warren, perhaps a relative, Speaker of the Virginia Assembly, to consider the conduct of Harvey. The next day the Governor called a meeting of his Council. His friend and Secretary of the Colony Richard Kemp writes:

"The Governor demanded if they had knowledge of the people's grievances. Mr. Minifie[1] answered that

[1] George Minifie arrived in the year 1623, in the ship Samuel. His plantation was between Blunt Point and Jamestown. De Vries visited in 1633, the James River and in his journal writes "Arrived at Littletown where Menifit lives. He has a garden of two acres full of primroses, apple, pear and cheery trees, the various fruits of Holland, with different kinds of sweet smelling herbs, rosemary, sage, marjoram,

their chiefest grievance was the not sending the answer of the late Assembly. The Governor rising from his place replied, 'Do you say so? I arrest you upon suspicion of treason to his Majesty.' Whereupon Captain Uty and Captain Mathews both of the Council laid hands upon the Governor using these words: 'And we, you, upon suspicion of treason to his Majesty.' The Council then demanded that he should go to England, to which he reluctantly consented, and on the 7th of May John West a brother of Lord Delaware was chosen acting Governor, and a Committee consisting of Uty and Peirce were sent to confer with the Governor of Maryland.

A correspondent of Thomas Wentworth, the Earl of Strafford, on August 19th, 1635, alludes to this difficulty, in these words:

"Sir John Harvey Governor of Virginia being invited on board of a ship, was suddenly carried away and is now brought into England. The company allege he was a Marylander, that is, one that favored too much my Lord Baltimore's Plantation, to their prejudice; but it is ill taken, that the Company of their own authority, should hurry him away in that manner."[1]

---

thyme. Around the house were planted peach trees which were hardly in bloom."

The Dutch Captain says that these were the first peach trees he saw in North America.

[1] Strafford Papers.

While the examination of Harvey was proceeding in England, Clayborne remained in undisturbed possession of Kent Island, until 1637, when he went to England leaving George Evelyn[1] in charge, who acknowledged the jurisdiction of Maryland, and Clay-

---

[1] The Evelyns and Calverts were of Flemish extraction. Sir John Evelyn had a son Robert of Goodstone Surrey who died before 1639, whose wife was Susan daughter of Gregory Young of York. George and Robert Evelyn were nephews of Capt. Thomas Young who was authorized on Sept. 22, 1633, by the King to fit out ships, appoint officers, and to make discoveries in America. Among the officers appointed were Robert Evelyn, a surgeon named Scott, and Alexander Baker of St. Holborn's parish, Middlesex, described by Young as "skillful in mines and trying of metals."

Stopping at Point Comfort for repairs and supplies, he left there on the 20th of July 1634, and on the 24th entered Delaware Bay. Slowly ascending the Delaware on the 22d of August he reached the Schuylkill, and after stopping five days again sailed, and on the 29th came to shoal water below the Falls.

Early in 1635 Lt. Robert Evelyn returned to England, and in 1637 appears again in America, and is appointed Surveyor of Virginia. His brother George probably came to Maryland at this time. At Piney Point on the Potomac George obtained a grant called the Manor of Evelynton and on April 3, 1638, entered lands for the following persons.

Thomas Hebden,	Daniel Wickliff,	Randall Revell,
James Cloughton,	Hugh Howard,	John Walker,
Henry Lee,	John Wortley,	John Richardson,
John Hill,	Wm. Medcalf,	Philip West,
Edmund Parris,	Howell Morgan,	Matthew Roedlen,
Roger Baxter,	Thomas Orley,	Wm. Williamson,
Thomas Keane,	Andrew Baker,	John Hatch.
Samuel Scovell,		

Through the Mynne family the Evelyns were related to the Calverts. Elizabeth Mynne, daughter of George Mynne, a relative of the wife of the first Lord Baltimore married a Richard Evelyn, and when she died in 1692, left the Manor of Horton, to Charles, 4th Lord Baltimore.

borne's goods were seized at Palmer's Island,[1] as well as this point. While the Maryland Assembly was confiscating his estate, Clayborne was not idle in London, and on the 4th of April, 1638, the Commissioners of Plantations reported the right and title to the Isle of Kent to be absolutely with him, and that the violence complained of, by him, to be left to the courts of justice."

The following note on the 14th of July was also sent to Cecil, Lord Baltimore: "The King understands that contrary to his pleasure, Lord Baltimore's agents have slain three persons, possessed themselves of the island by force, and seized the persons and estates of

---

[1] Among others, the following were taken by Lord Baltimore's agents at Palmer's Island.

Servants.

Edward Griffin, William Jones,
Richard Roymont, William Freeman.

Books.

A Statute Book.
Five or Six Little Books.
One Great Book of Mr. Perkins.

The latter may have been one of the volumes sent out from London. At a meeting of the Virginia Company on November 15, 1620, as the reading of the minutes was finished, "a stranger stepped in" and presented a map of Sir Walter Raleigh's, containing a description of Guiana, and with the same, four Great Books, as the gift of one who desired his name might not be known. Three of these folios were the works of Perkins the distinguished divine of Cambridge University. The donor desired these books might be sent to the college in Virginia, there to remain in safety to the use of the collegiate educators, and not suffered at any time to be lent abroad. See *History of Virginia Company*, published by Munsell, Albany, page 197.

the planters. These disorders have been referred to the Commissioners for Plantations. He is therefore commanded to allow the planters and their agents to have free enjoyment of their possessions without further trouble, until the cause is decided."

In the year 1644, between October and Christmas, with a party of men from Chicacoan in Virginia, Clayborne took possession of Kent Isle but did not remain, and in 1646 came again with forty persons under a commission from Governor Berkeley of Virginia, but in the next year was compelled to retire.

During these troubles Sir Edmund Plowden, who as early as July 1632, had obtained a patent for Long Isle, and forty leagues between 39 and 40 degrees of north latitude was visiting Virginia and Maryland, and in the "Description of the Province of New Albion," published in 1648, speaks of "Captain Claiborne, heretofore Secretary now Treasurer of Virginia," and adds:

"Now Kent Isle, was with many households of English, by Captain Clayborn before seated, and because his Majesty by his privy signet shortly after declared that it was not his intention to grant any lands before seated and habited, and for that, it lyeth by the Maryland printed card, clear northward, within Albion and not in Maryland, and not only late Seamen, but old depositions in Clayborn's hand shows it to be out of Maryland, and for that Albion's privy signet is elder and before Maryland patent, Clayborn by force entered and thrust Master Calvert out of Kent."[1]

In 1640, we find that Clayborne had returned to America, and on the 20th of June petitioned the Virginia authorities for 3000 acres of land at the town of Patomack where in 1622 the English had built a fort, which was on the Virginia side of the Potomac, a few miles from Potopaco, Maryland.

The beheading of King Charles by the Parliament of England led to a compromise with the Virginians. In 1652 William Clayborne and Richard Bennett as Commissioners of Parliament removed Lord Baltimore's officers in Maryland and appointed others, in the name of the keepers of the liberty of England. For five years he performed the duties of Commissioner, and after this period lived at the junction of the York and Pamunkey on the site of the Indian village Candayack, now called West Point. In Herrman's Map prepared for Lord Baltimore, and published in 1673, the neck of land is called Clayborne. After the

[1] In 1632 Plowden and others petitioned for Long Isle or Isle Plowden, and other isles between 39th and 40th degree of north latitude, with 40 leagues square of adjoining continent to be granted " a County Palatine or body politic by the name of New Albion." The King, on the 24th of July, ordered the letters patent to be granted. See *Strafford's Letters*, vol. I, pp. 72, 73. In Hazard's Annals of Pennsylvania there is a deposition that Sir Edmund Plowden, residing in Virginia in 1643, bought of Philip White of Kiquotan, the half of a bark. He returned to England, was imprisoned for debt and died A.D. 1655.

restoration of Charles the Second, he was again honored with the Secretaryship of Virginia, which he had first held about forty years before, and in 1666 was chosen a member of the legislature. The time of his death has not been ascertained. His son Thomas was killed by the Indians, and his tombstone a few years ago was visible. The Quaker preacher, Thomas Story, speaks of visiting, in 1699, William Clayborne of Pamunkey Neck, who was probably another son of the old Virginia Secretary, and Parliament Commissioner.

EMBARCATION OF MARYLAND COLONISTS.

WE are now prepared to notice the pioneers of Lord Baltimore's Plantation in Maryland. It has been al ready stated, that the Privy Council, after hearing the arguments of the Virginia planters, ordered, on July 3d, 1633, that Lord Baltimore should be left to his patent, and the Virginians "to the course of law, according to their desire." A number of friends joined with Cecil Lord Baltimore, in fitting out an expedition On the 31st of the same month, in which the decision of the Council was announced, the following order was issued by that body.

"Whereas the good ship called the Ark of Maryland of the burthen of about 350 tons, whereof one Lowe is Master, is set forth by our very good Lord, the Lord Baltimore for his Lordship's plantation at Maryland in America and manned with about 40 men. Forasmuch as his Lordship hath desired, that the men belonging to his said ship, may be free from press or interruption, these are to will and require you, to forbear to take up, or press any, the officers, seamen, mariners or others belonging to his Lordship's said ship either in her voyage to Maryland, or in her return for England,

and that you permit and suffer her quietly to pass and return without any let or hindrance, stay or interruption whatsoever."[1] A pinnace of twenty tons, commanded by Captain Winter, called The Dove, accompanied the Ark.

On the 19th of October, Coke the Secretary of State,[2] informed Admiral Penington "that the Ark, Richard Lowe[3] Master, carrying men for Lord Baltimore to his new plantation in or about New England, had sailed from Gravesend contrary to orders, the company in charge of Capt. Winter[4] not having taken the oath of allegiance,"[5] and directed him to have the expedition

---

[1] Copied from original in British Public Record Office.

[2] Sainsbury's State Papers.

[3] In the M'd Assembly of 1638 was Richard Loe probably the same person. He died in 1639 and John Lewger, the first Secretary of the Province, was his executor. He bequeathed to Lewger's wife, "a satin petticoat." See Annapolis MSS.

[4] A Capt. Robert Winter was in the Assembly of 1638. On January 12, 1637–38, he transported the following servants, Richard Browne, Arthur Webb, John Speed, Bartholomew Phillips, Thomas White, Rowland Morgan, George Tailor, aged 15 years. Before September 1638 he died. See Annapolis MSS.

[5] Pope Pius the Fifth had freed English subjects, from allegiance to the Sovereign of England. After the Gun Powder Plot the Oath of Allegiance was required of all persons sailing to English colonies. It begins as follows.

"I A—— B—— do truly and sincerely acknowledge, profess, testify, and declare in my conscience before God and the World, that our Sovereign Lord King James is lawful and righteous King of this realm, and all other his Majesty's dominions and countries, and that the Pope, neither of himself, nor by any authority by the Church or See of Rome, or by any other means with any other, hath any power or authority to depose the King, or to dispose of any of his Majesty's

brought back. After the vessels were again anchored, near Gravesend, they were visited by Edward Watkins the London Searcher, who reported to the Privy Council as follows: "According to your Lordship's order of the 25th day of this instant month of October, I have been at Tillbury Hope where I found a ship and pinnace belonging to the Right Honorable Cecil Lord Baltimore where I offered the oath of allegiance to all and every the persons aboard, to the number of about 128, who took the same, and inquiring of the Master of the Ship whether any more persons were to go the said voyage, he answered that some few others were shipped who had forsaken the ship and given over the voyage, by reason of the stay of said ships."[1]

The vessels after they left the Thames stopped at the Isle of Wight, where the Jesuit Father White, and others who had forsaken the ship, were probably received. On the 22d of November they sailed from this Isle. Father White writes: "Yet we were not without apprehension, for the sailors were murmuring among themselves, saying that they were expecting a

---

kingdoms or dominions," etc. Another clause reads: "Also I do swear from my heart, that notwithstanding any declaration or sentence of excommunication, or deprivation made or granted by the Pope or his successors * * * * * * I will bear faith and true allegiance to his Majesty," etc. Again "And I do believe, and in conscience am resolved, that neither the Pope, nor any person whatsoever, hath power to absolve me of this oath," etc.

[1] Copy, from original, in British Public Record Office.

messenger with letters from London, and from this it seemed as if they were ever contriving to delay us."

After the ships had been at sea several weeks, Cecil Lord Baltimore wrote to his deceased father's intimate friend, Wentworth, known in history as Earl of Strafford, the following account of the difficulties of sending out the first ships to his Plantation:

"After many difficulties since your Lordship's departure from hence, in the proceedings of my Plantation wherein I felt your Lordship's absence, I have at last sent away my ships, and have deferred my going till another time, and indeed my Lord, my ships are gone; after having been so many ways troubled by my adversaries, after they had endeavored to overthrow my business at the Council Board, after they had informed by several means some of the Lords of the Council that I intended to carry over nuns into Spain, and soldiers to serve that King, which I believe your Lordship will laugh at, as well they did, after they had gotten Mr. Attorney General to make an information in the Star-Chamber that my ships were departed from Gravesend without any cockets from the Custom House, and in contempt of all authority, my people abusing the King's officers, and refusing to take the oath of allegiance; whereupon their Lordships sent present order to several captains of the King's ships who lay in the Downs, to search for my ships in the river, and to follow them into the narrow seas, if they were gone out, and to bring them back to Gravesend, which they did, and all this done before I knew anything of it, but imagined all the while that my ships were well advanced on their voyage; but not to trouble your Lordship with too many circumstances, I, as soon as I had notice of it, made it plainly appear unto their Lordships, that Mr. Attorney was abused and misinformed, and that there was not any just cause of complaint in any of the former accusations, and that every one of them was most notoriously and maliciously false, whereupon they were pleased to restore my ships to their former liberty.

"After they had likewise corrupted and seduced my mariners, and defamed the business all they could by their scandalous reports, I have as I said, at last, by the help of some of your Lordship's good friends and mine, overcome these difficulties, and sent a hopeful colony into Maryland with a fair and probable expectation of good success, however without any danger of any great prejudice unto myself, in respect that others are joined with me in the adventure. There are two of my brothers gone, with very near twenty other gentlemen of very good fashion, and three hundred laboring men well provided in all things."[1]

The following were the few persons above the condition of laboring men:

[1] Strafford's Letters.

Leonard Calvert, Governor.	Frederick Winter.
Thomas Cornwallis, Commissioner.	John Saunders.
Jerome Hawley,	Thomas Dorrell.
Andrew White, Priest.	Edward Cranfield.
John Altham, alias Gravener, Priest.	Capt. John Hill.
George Calvert, Baltimore's brother.	Henry Green.
Justinian Snow, Factor.	John Medcalf.
Henry Wiseman.	Nicholas Fairfax.
Richard Gerard.	William Saire.
Edward Winter.	John Baxter.

Fairfax and others died before they reached their destination, others survived but a little while after landing, and some left the Plantation.

Saunders, the partner of Cornwallis in business, died soon after arrival in Maryland, the brothers of Sir John Winter lived but two or three years,[1] George Calvert went to Virginia and was in sympathy with Clayborne, and died before the year 1653,[2] Richard Gerard who was about twenty years of age when he landed at St. Mary, remained in America about one year. During the civil war in England he adhered to the King and was Governor of Denbigh Castle. After the restoration of monarchy, he was made one of the cup bearers of Charles the Second.[3]

[1] Annapolis MSS.

[2] In the statement of Lord Baltimore's Case, published in London in 1653, it is stated, that both of his brothers, Leonard and George Calvert, had died in America.

[3] Foster's Lancashire.

GOVERNOR LEONARD CALVERT.

THE Government of the Plantation was entrusted by Cecil, Lord Baltimore, to his brother Leonard Calvert as Deputy, with two commissioners, Thomas Cornwallis and Jerome Hawley, as friends and advisers.

Leonard Calvert was the second son of George Calvert the first Lord Baltimore, born about A.D., 1606, and thus twenty-eight years of age at the time of his landing at Saint Mary. In early life he had lived in Ireland, and in the spring of 1629 under a letter of marque, sailed in the ship St. Claude for Newfoundland, and it was in this ship probably, that his father and family went to Virginia, in the autumn of that year.[1]

His life as Governor of Maryland was not distinguished for boldness and originality, and his relative George Evelyn the Commander of Kent Island once sneeringly said, "Who was his grandfather but a grazier? what was his father? what was Leonard Calvert himself at school but a dunce and a blockhead."[2]

He appears to have been greatly under the influence of Margaret Brent, a strong-minded woman, who on

[1] See Page 42.

[2] Streeter's Evelyn.

November 22, 1638, arrived in Maryland with her sister Mary, and brothers Fulk and Giles.

Cecil Lord Baltimore, in 1639 was so poor, that he and his wife and children were obliged to live at the house of his father-in-law, Earl Arundel,[1] and his brother Leonard, when he died on the 9th of June 1647, was far from rich.

His successor as the head of the Province, Thomas Green, has left on record an interesting statement of the last events of his life. About six hours before he expired, in Green's presence he said to Margaret Brent, "I make you my sole executor. Take all, and pay all." After these words he desired all to leave the room, but Margaret with whom he had private conference. When Green was again invited to his bed-side, he heard him say "I give my wearing clothes to James Lindsay and Richard William my servants, specifying his cloth suit to Richard William, and his black suit to James Lindsay, and his wearing linen to be divided between them. I give my colt to my godson Leonard Green," and also requested that the first mare colt that should fall, be given to Mrs. Temperance Pypott of Virginia."[2]

Under this nuncupative will, Margaret Brent claimed and held the house in which Governor Calvert resided.

---

[1] Bruce's State Papers.

[2] Annapolis Manuscripts.

Recognized by the Maryland Assembly of 1648, as the attorney of Governor Calvert, she demanded a vote in that body, against which Governor Green protested. With masculine vigor, she then claimed to be the representative of the Lord Proprietary, and, in turn, protested against all the acts of the Assembly.

Lord Baltimore was displeased at her position and wrote "bitter invectives," but the Assembly of 1649, defended her, with a gallantry worthy of the courtiers of Queen Elizabeth. They stated to the Proprietary in England: "As for Mistress Brent's undertaking, and meddling with your estate, we do verily believe, and in conscience report, that it was better for the colony's safety, at that time, in her hands, than in any man's else,[1] in the whole Province, after your brother's death; for the soldiers would never have treated any other with that civility and respect, and though they was ever ready at several times to run into mutiny, yet she still pacified them, till at last things were brought to that strait, that she must be admitted and declared your Lordship's attorney, by order of Court."

In the early records, there is a notice of this lady journeying, in May, 1643, to the Isle of Kent, accompanied by Anne a lame maid servant of Sir Edmund Plowden. Until late in life, the Attorney of

[1] The expression "any *man's* else" may be a slip of the pen, not a p un.

Leonard Calvert retained her powers of fascination. When fifty-seven years old, in 1658, she states to the Provincial Court, "that Thomas White lately deceased out of the tender love and affection he bore unto the petitioner, intended if he had lived to have married her, and did by his last will give unto the said petitioner his whole estate which he was possessed of in his life time."[1] Three years after this, she was alive, but the precise date of the death of Leonard Calvert's best friend, has not been ascertained.

[1] Annapolis Manuscripts.

THOMAS CORNWALLIS, COMMISSIONER.

COMMISSIONER Thomas Cornwallis was the most prominent of the founders of Maryland. In mental endowments, well known ancestry, and worldly goods, he had no superior.

His grandfather was Sir Charles Cornwallis,[1] distin-

[1] CORNWALLIS PEDIGREE.

Sir THOMAS CORNWALLIS, Kt. Comptroller of the Household of Queen Mary. Married Anne daughter of Sir John Jerningham. Died 1604. Had two sons, and three daughters.

Sir WILLIAM.

Sir CHARLES. Knighted by King James and Ambassador to Spain. Married Elizabeth dau. of Thomas Fincham, Esq. Had two sons.

Sir WILLIAM, Kt., married Catharine daughter of Sir Philip Parker of Erwarton, Suffolk. Had six sons and five daughters.

THOMAS, married Anne dau. of Samuel Bevercott of Ordsall near Scrooby, and probably sister of Sam'l the postmaster of Scrooby, before William Brewster who became the head of the first Puritan colony in America.

THOMAS, 2d son, Com'r of Maryland.

A brother of the Maryland Commissioner was Rector of a Suffolk Parish, and on a brass tablet in the church is a Latin inscription which translated reads :

"Here are placed the remains of the holy man Philip Cornwaleys, former Rector of this Church, youngest son of William Cornwaleys, Knight. Died Dec. 30, 1688."

In the grave yard there is a stone in memory of "Frances wife of Samuel Richardson, Clerk, daughter of Thomas Cornwallis Esq., died June 24, 1684," who was probably the aunt of the Maryland Commissioner.

guished as the English Ambassador at the court of Spain, and subsequently as the Treasurer of King James' son, Henry, Prince of Wales. In 1614, he fell under the displeasure of the King, because he sympathized with certain members of Parliament, who were opposed to the marriage of Prince Charles with a daughter of the King of France, and the suppression of faithful Puritan ministers.

His father Sir William, K't, was noted for his literary tastes, and printed essays. The Commissioner was born in 1603, and was thirty-one years of age, when he landed on the shores of the Potomac.

In 1635, he commanded the expedition against the Virginians, trading in the Chesapeake.[1]

After Evelyn became Commander of Kent Island, on Dec. 3d, 1637, he was licensed to trade with the Indians, and shipped in the pinnace St. Thomas for that island, axes, and other articles in the name of his fellow commissioner Jerome Hawley.

The Charter of Maryland conferred monarchical power upon the Proprietary. It authorized him to prepare laws, and submit them to any legislature convened, and dissolved at his pleasure. In 1637, Lord Baltimore instructed Governor Calvert to call a legislature, and present a code of laws sent out from England, for their acceptance. In January, 1638, the Assembly convened pursuant to notice. The Governor,

[1] See page 51.

and Secretary Lewger,[1] although but few members were present, desired that the laws prepared by the Proprietary should be assented to after a single reading, to which Cornwallis objected. The Governor continued to press the question, but when the vote was taken, a large majority refused, at that time, to accept the laws. After a brief adjournment, the assembly met in February, and the delegates then resolved that all laws should be read three times on three several days, before a vote should be taken, and they also expressed a wish that all bills might emanate from their own committee. Governor Calvert, restive at the independence of the members, again proposed to adjourn, which Cornwallis described in a pamphlet of the day as "that noble, right valiant, and politic sol-

---

[1] Wood in *Athenæ Oxoniensis* states that John Lewger, the first Secretary of the Province was born in London 1602 and took the degree of A.B. in 1619 at Trinity College, Oxford, and in 1622 was made A.M. Became a Bachelor of Divinity on the same day as Phil. Nye, the prominent member of the Westminster Assembly of Divines. In 1632 he was a Rector of the Church of England in Essex, but under the influence of Chillingworth became a Roman Catholic, and soon after, Chillingworth renounced the Church of Rome and wrote a book in which he states: "The Bible, and that only, is the religion of Protestants, and every one by making use of the helps and assistances that God has placed in his hands, must learn that, and understand it for himself, as well as he can."

Lewger after joining the Roman Church was appointed by his college classmate Cecil, Lord Baltimore, Secretary of Maryland and in November 1637 arrived with his wife, and son John aged nine years, Martha Williamson a maid servant, and several others.

The Annapolis Records mention Cicely and Elizabeth Lewger who were probably born in the Province. The wife of the Secretary died

dier" opposed, and said "that they could not spend their time in any business better than this for the country's good."

The Governor replied that he would be accountable to no man, and adjourned the Assembly until the 5th of March. The freemen then convened and after passing such Acts as they approved, on the 19th, the Assembly was dissolved.

Lord Baltimore now receded from his arbitrary position, and told his brother that he would assent to all laws enacted by the Provincial legislature, not contrary to the laws of England, subject to the final approval of the Proprietary.

The next legislature convened in February 1639, and enacted the law of England "that Holy Church shall have and enjoy all her rights, liberties and fran-

---

in a few years, and soon after the civil war broke out under Ingle he went back to England and never returned. Being a widower he entered the priesthood and lived at Lord Baltimore's house in London. Benjamin Denham, the Earl of Winchester's Chaplain in 1667 writes: "All that is treated of in the Privy Council about Roman Catholics is discovered to Lord Brudenell, and Lord Baltimore, Governor of Maryland, whose Chaplain, an English recusant, now a Romish priest, was one of the vice-gerents there in Charles the First's time."—*Green's State Papers*. He died about this period.

John Lewger Jr. remained in the Province, and when twenty years of age, acted as temporary clerk of the Assembly of 1647–48. By profession he was a Surveyor. On August 28th, 1650, he secured the house which had been his Father's at Saint Mary. In his will dated Nov. 6, 1669, he alludes to his "loving wife Martha," his sons William and John, and gives his daughter Elizabeth "his cow Muley."— *See Annapolis Manuscripts.*

chises wholly and without blemish" which Church under the charter, was the Church of England.

Soon after Cornwallis had finished a substantial brick house, the best in the colony, in 1640, he visited England, and in December, 1641, returned to Maryland, in a ship, commanded by Captain Richard Ingle, and took his seat in the legislature which in March, 1642, was convened.

The very first step of this Assembly was to declare that it could not be adjourned without its consent, another advance in the direction of republicanism.

The next year an order was issued to the Colonial Surveyor "to lay out 4000 acres of land in any part of Patowmack river upward of Port Tobacco creek, for Capt. Cornwaleys."

Owing to an order for reorganization of the government received from Lord Baltimore, Governor Calvert convened an Assembly on the 5th of September 1642. Under the reconstruction, Cornwallis was designated as a Councillor but "he absolutely refused to take the oath of a Councillor according to the requirements of the last commission."

In the spring of 1643, Leonard Calvert sailed for England and Giles Brent became acting Governor, who commissioned Cornwallis to lead an expedition against the Susquehanna Indians. The author of Nova Albion writes, that with fifty-three "raw and tired

Marylanders" he met two hundred and fifty Indians and killed twenty-nine.

In November 1643, a London ship commanded by Richard Ingle sailed for America. Upon its arrival at Saint Mary, by virtue of a commission granted by Charles the First, acting Governor Brent captured the vessel, Ingle escaping, and tendered the crew an oath against Parliament. In January 1644, he summoned Ingle to yield his body to the Sheriff of Saint Mary County to answer for treason against his Majesty, but he did not appear, and left the Province.

When the war between the King and Parliament commenced, Cornwallis was living with more comfort and elegance than any one in Maryland. In his own language: "By God's blessing upon his endeavors, he had acquired a settled and comfortable subsistence having a comfortable dwelling house furnished with plate, linen hangings, bedding, brass, pewter, and all manner of household stuff, worth at least a thousand pounds, about twenty servants, at least a hundred breed cattle, a great stock of swine and goats, some sheep and horses, a new pinnace about twenty tons, well rigged and fitted, besides a new shallop and other small boats."

Appointing Cuthbert Fenwick his agent he sailed for England in April, 1644, where he found his cousin Sir Frederick Cornwallis one of the best friends of King Charles, and Governor Leonard Calvert who did not return to Maryland until the following September.

Ingle, smarting under the seizure of his ship, was commissioned by Parliament, to cruise in the waters of the Chesapeake, against malignants as the friends of the King were called, and in February 1645, appearep in the ship Reformation, near St. Inigo creek, when there was an uprising in favor of Parliament, in which all the servants of Cornwallis participated, except some negroes and a tailor named Richard Hervey-Fenwick, his agent, was taken aboard Ingle's ship, and a party led by John Sturman, his son Thomas, and William Hardwick took possession of the mansion, burned the fences, killed the swine, took the cattle, wrenched off the locks from the doors, and damaged his estate to the amount of two or three thousand pounds. When Ingle returned to England with Father White the Jesuit as a prisoner, Cornwallis, who was there, instituted a suit against him, which called forth in February, 1646, the following memorial to the Lords in Parliament assembled.

"The humble petition of Richard Ingle, showing That whereas the petitioner, having taken the covenant, and going out with letters of marque, as Captain of the ship the Reformation, of London, and sailing to Maryland, where, finding the Governor of that Province to have received a commission from Oxford to seize upon all ships belonging to London, and to execute a tyrannical power against the Protestants, and such as adhered to the Parliament, and to press wicked oaths upon them, and to endeavor their extirpation, the petitioner, conceiving himself, not only by his warrant, but in his fidelity to the Parliament, to be conscientiously obliged to come to their assistance, did venture his life and fortune in landing his men and assisting the said well affected Protestants against the said tyrannical government and the Papists and malignants. It pleased God to enable him to take divers places from them, and to make him a support to the said well affected. But since his return to England, the said Papists and malignants, conspiring together, have brought fictitious acts against him, at the common law, in the name of Thomas Cornwallis and others, for pretended trespass in taking away their goods, in the parish of St. Christopher's, London, which are the very goods that were by force of war justly and lawfully taken from these wicked Papists and malignants in Maryland, and with which he relieved the poor distressed Protestants there, who otherwise must have starved, and been rooted out.

"Now, forasmuch as your Lordships in Parliament of State, by the order annexed, were pleased to direct an ordinance to be framed for the settlement of the said province of Maryland, under the Committee of Plantations, and for the indemnity of the actors in it, and for that such false and feigned actions for matters of war acted in foreign parts, are not tryable at common law, but, if at all, before the Court and Marshall; and for that it would be a dangerous example to permit Papists and malignants to bring actions of trespass or otherwise against the well affected for fighting and standing for the Parliament:

"The petitioner most humbly beseecheth your Lordships to be pleased to direct that this business may be heard before your Lordships at the bar, or to refer it to a committee to report the true state of the case, and to order that the said suits against the petitioner at the common law may be staid, and no further proceeded in."

For eight years Cornwallis attended to business in London, and in 1652 returned to Maryland, now under the control of the friends of Parliament, to demand compensation for injuries done by certain persons to his property, during the Ingle revolution. To secure the amount of land due to him, for the transportation of servants, the following memorandum was filed.

SERVANTS BROUGHT A.D. 1634,

Twelve in the Ark, besides five more received by the death of his partner, John Saunders.

The same year brought from Virginia

Cuthbert Fenwick.[1]	John Norton, Sr.[3]
Christopher Martin.[2]	John Norton, Jr.

[1] Member of Assembly 1638, and other years.
[2] A tailor; Assemblyman in 1638.
[3] Assemblyman in 1638.

A.D. 1635.

Zachary Mottershead.[1]
John Gage,[2]
Walter Waterling.[2]
Francis Van Eyden.

A.D. 1636.

John Cook.
Tho. York, killed at Nantioke.
Daniel Clocker.[2]
Richard Hill.
Restitutia Tue.[3]

A.D. 1637.

Charles Maynard.
Stephen Gray.
Francis Shirley.
Ann Wiggin.
Alice Moreman.[4]

A. D. 1639.

Nicholas Gwyther.[5]
Edmund Jaques.
Richard Farmer.
Edmund Deering.
George, a tailor.
William Freak.
Morris Freeman.
Jeremiah Coote,
Martha Jackson.

A.D. 1640.

William Durford.
Henry Brooke.
George, a Smith.
Edward Matthews.
Hannah Ford.

---

[1] Assemblyman in 1638.

[2] Signer of Protestant Declaration in 1648.

[3] Married in 1639 to John Hollis.

[4] Married in 1639 to Francis Gray, carpenter, who was in Assembly, of 1638.

[5] Sheriff of St. Mary County.

A.D. 1641.

Francis Anthill.
Richard Harvey.[1]
Charles Rawlinson.
Richard Harris.
Thomas Harrison.
Edward Ward.
Robert King.
Mary Phillips.
John Wheatley.
Wheatley's wife.

A.D. 1642.

Thomas Rockwood.
John Rockwood.
Elizabeth Batte.

A.D. 1646.

Magdalene Wittle.

A.D. 1651.

Robert Curtis.
William Sinckleare.
Thomas Frisell.
William Wells.
John Maylande.
John Eston.
Sarah Lindle.

In another memorandum he mentions the following persons:

A.D. 1633–34.

John Hallowes.
John Holden.
Josias, drowned.
Roger Walter.
Roger Morgan.

A.D. 1635.

William Penshoot.
Richard Cole.
John Medley.[2]
Richard Brown.
Richard Brock.

In a memorial to the Assembly of Maryland Corn-

[1] A tailor.
[2] In Legislature A.D., 1647.

wallis uses this language: "It is well known, he hath at his great cost and charges, from the first planting of this Province for the space of twenty-eight years, been one of the greatest propagators and increasers thereof, by the yearly transportation of servants, whereof divers have been of very good rank and quality, towards whom and the rest he hath always been so careful to discharge a good conscience, in the true performance of his promise and obligations, that he was never taxed with any breach thereof, though it is also well known and he doth truly aver it, that the charge of so great a family, as he hath always maintained was never defrayed by their labor."[1]

He appears now to be making arrangements for building on the point of the Potomac, above Potopaco. A contract was made on November 23, 1652, with Cornelius Canada brickmaker, and former servant of Governor Green, to deliver thirty-six thousand sound, well burned bricks, before a certain day in June, 1653, and another twenty-four thousand before the 24th of June, 1654.[2]

In 1654, he again visited England, and before he returned, was married to a young maiden, Penelope, daughter of John Wiseman of Middle Temple, and Tyrrels, in county Essex.[3] The marriage probably

[1] Annapolis Manuscripts.

[2] *Private Correspondence of Jane, Lady Cornwallis*, 1613–1664. London, 1842.

took place in 1657, his wife at that time being twenty-one years of age.

In 1658 he appears in Maryland with his young wife, and early in 1659, left, never to return. His affairs in the Province, were entrusted to an attorney, and he began to be designated as a " merchant of London."

In Norfolk County, England, there is a place called Maryland Point, named by a retired American merchant who built a house there, and that person is supposed to have been Thomas Cornwallis of Burnham Thorpe, the best and wisest of the founders of Maryland. He died in 1676 at the age of seventy-two, leaving a widow forty years of age, by whom he had four sons and six daughters.

His second son Thomas born in 1662, just after his mother's return from Maryland, was a clergyman of the Church of England, and died in 1731, Rector of a parish in Suffolk.

A son of the Suffolk Rector, William, born in 1708, also became a clergyman and died in 1746, Rector of Chelmondester, Suffolk.

William's son, William, born in 1751, followed in the footsteps of his father and grandfather and became Rector of Wittersham and Elam, Kent. His wife Mary was a woman of piety and culture, and published " Observations on the canonical Scriptures," the last edition of which was published in 1828, in four volumes.

His daughter Caroline Frances, was a Greek and

Hebrew scholar, poetess, brilliant writer, and friend of Sismondi. She wrote the article on *Wycliffe and his Times*, in the Westminster Review of July 1854, and on the *Capabilities and Disabilities of Woman*, in January 1857, and was the authoress of *Pericles, a tale of Athens*, a *Prize Essay on Juvenile Delinquency*, and a series of valuable works on physiology, Greek philosophy, and the development of Christian doctrine and practice, published as *Small Books on Great Subjects.*[1]

She died unmarried in 1858, the last descendant of Thomas, the second son of the prudent Commissioner of Maryland.

[1] *Letters of Caroline Frances Cornwallis,* London, 1864.

JEROME HAWLEY, COMMISSIONER.

JEROME Hawley was the joint commissioner with Cornwallis, in settling the Province of Maryland. He was the son of James Hawley of Brentford near London, and seems when a young man to have had some connection with the trial of the dissolute wife of the Earl of Somerset, for conspiring to poison the poet Sir Thomas Overbury, the nephew of the person after whom Palmer's Island, in the Susquehanna, was named. Among the British State Papers, there is an order to the commissioners in the Overbury Case, from King James, dated November 25, 1615, directing that "Jerome son of James Hawley now close prisoner in the Gate House, be released, on condition of his not going farther than his father's house at Brentford.[1]

About this time, Jerome Hawley reported that Sir John Leeds and wife declared, that the King "was unwieldy, could not unlock a door, but might jump out of the window," and Lady Leeds further said, she would speak treason, because the King said "most women were atheists or papists."[2]

[1] Green State Papers. [2] Green State Papers.

After the accession of Charles the First to the throne, he was one of the sewers or superintendent of the banquets of Queen Henrietta Maria.

His brother Henry, by the influence of the Puritan Earl of Warwick, became Governor of Barbadoes in 1636, and while he was visiting England in 1638 another brother, William, acted as Deputy.[1]

After Cornwallis killed some of the Virginians in Maryland waters, Jerome Hawley immediately sailed for England to defend the action of his fellow commissioner, and in June 1635 arrived in London, and appeared before the Privy Council. He remained there for a long period, and on the 27th of June 1636, proposed to meet the King at Court, on the next Sunday, to make some proposals relative to the tobacco trade, and on the 4th of August, an order was issued to the Governor and Council of Virginia, that all tobacco should be consigned to London in English ships, and duly inspected. Early the next year, Jerome Hawley was appointed to receive the annual rent of twelve pence, upon every fifty acres of land granted in Virginia, and was made Treasurer of the Colony. Arriving at Jamestown he took the oath of allegiance, and entered upon his duties.

On February 26, 1638, one George Reade writes to his brother, a clerk of Secretary Windebank: "Mr.

[1] Sainsbury Papers.

Hawley has not proved the man he took him for, having neither given any satisfaction for money, received of him, nor brought him any servants."

In the summer of 1638 Treasurer Hawley died, and Thomas Cornwallis was the administrator of his estate. From the account of administration rendered on April 20, 1639, it is evident that Hawley was poor. His brother William, removed from Barbadoes, and in 1650, was one of the signers of the Protestant Declaration. The following letter of James, another brother of Jerome living at Brentford has been preserved,[1] addressed to Captain William Hawley.

"Loving Brother: I received lately a letter from you dated the 26th of February last, by which, to understand of your good health doth much gladden me. As concerning your intent for Maryland I do like well of it, and do herewith send you the copy of writings betwixt my brother Jerome deceased, and myself from which will appear a large sum of money to be due unto me, from him, which by virtue of my power of attorney, I do authorize you to receive in my behalf.

"Upon the decease of my brother Jerome, one Cornwallis did seize upon his estate, pretending that he was indebted unto him, but I am informed it was only a doubtful pretence, to defraud me.

"If by your means, anything may be gotten, I will

[1] Annapolis Manuscripts.

assist you for the present. My brother Henry, hath promised to procure a letter from my Lord Baltimore, in your behalf, which will be much to your advantage. As concerning the Statute, I send you only a copy thereof at present, but if it will be useful to you, you may have the original sent unto you, when you require it. You must pretend your own right as next heir to brother Jerome, as well as my interest, for indeed there is only one daughter of his, before you, which is at Brabant, and mindeth not the same.

So with my hearty desire of your good prosperity and welfare, at present cease, resting ever

Your loving brother,

JAMES HAWLEY.

Brentford, Co. Middlesex, 30th of July, 1649.

RELIGION IN THE PROVINCE, UNTIL THE EXECUTION OF CHARLES THE FIRST.

ON the 29th of October, 1632, in consequence of a rumor that persons were on board, who had scruples of conscience against the oath of allegiance, Edward Hawkins, a Searcher of London, visited the Ark and the Dove, and administered the following Oath, to all whom he found.

"I do truly and sincerely acknowledge, profess, testify, and declare in my conscience, before God and the world;

"That our Sovereign Lord, King Charles, is lawful and rightful King of this realm, and of all other his Majesty's dominions and countrie, and that the Pope neither of himself, nor by any authority by the Church, or See of Rome, or by any other means with any other, hath any power or authority to depose the King, or to dispose of any of his Majesty's Kingdoms or dominions; or to authorize any foreign Prince, to invade or annoy him or his countries; or to discharge any of his subjects of their allegiance, and obedience to his Majesty; or to give license or leave to any of them to bear arms, raise tumults, or to offer any violence or hurt, to his

Majesty's royal person, state, or government, or to any of his Majesty's subjects within his Majesty's domains.

"And I do swear from my heart, that notwithstanding any declaration, or sentence of excommunication, or deprivation, made or granted by the Pope, or his successors, or by any authority derived, or pretended to be derived from him, or his See, against the said King, his heir or successors, or any absolution of the said subjects from their obedience, I will bear faith and true allegiance to his Majesty, his heirs and successors, and him and them will defend to the uttermost of my power, against all conspiracies and attempts whatsoever, which shall be made against his or their persons, their crown and dignity, by reason or color of any such sentence, or declaration, or otherwise; and will do my best endeavor to disclose and make known unto his Majesty, his heirs and successors, all treasons, or traitorous conspiracies, which I shall know or hear of, to be against him or any of them.

"And I do further swear, that I do from my heart, abhor, detest, and abjure, as impious and heretical, this damnable doctrine and position; that, Princes which be excommunicated or deprived by the Pope, may be deposed or murthered by their subjects, or any other whatsoever.

"And I do believe, and in conscience am resolved, that neither the Pope, nor any person whatsoever, hath power to absolve me of this Oath, or any part thereof, which I acknowledge by good and full authority to be lawfully ministered unto me, and do renounce all pardons, and dispensations to the contrary. And all these things I do plainly and sincerely acknowledge and swear, according to these express words by me spoke, and according to the plain, and common sense and understanding of the same words, without any equivocation or mental evasion, or secret reservation whatsoever. And I do make this recognition and acknowledgment heartily, willingly, and truly upon the true faith of a Christian: So help me God."

After this oath was taken, the vessels proceeded to the Isle of Wight, when Father White and others who had not taken the oath, had an opportunity to come aboard. White, in his Journal, published by the Maryland Historical Society, thus describes the sailing of Lord Baltimore's colony, for America.

"On the twenty-second of November, in the year 1633, being St. Cecilia's day, we set sail from Cowes, in the Isle of Wight, with a gentle east wind blowing. And after committing the principal parts of the ship to the protection of God especially, and of His most Holy Mother, and St. Ignatius, we sailed on a little way between the two shores, and the wind failing us, we stopped opposite Yarmouth Castle, which is near the southern end of the same island.

"Here we were received with a cheerful salute of artillery. Yet we were not without apprehension, for the sailors were murmuring among themselves, saying that they were expecting a messenger with letters from London, and from this it seemed as if they were even contriving to delay us. But God brought their plans to confusion, for that very night a favorable but strong wind arose, and a French cutter, which had put into the same harbor with us, being forced to set sail, came near running into our pinnace. The latter, therefore, to avoid being run down, having cut away and lost an anchor, set sail without delay, and since it was dangerous to drift about in that place, made haste to get further out to sea. And so, that we might not lose sight of our pinnace, we determined to follow. Thus the designs of the sailors who were plotting against us, were frustrated. This happened on the 23d of November, St. Clement's day."

Father White also states, that "if you except the usual sea-sickness, no one was attacked by any disease, until the festival of the nativity of our Lord.

"In order that the day might be better kept, wine was given out, and those who drank of it too freely were seized the next day with a fever, and of these not long afterwards, about twelve died, of whom two were Catholics."

Newport, the commander of the first expedition for the settlement of Virginia, planted a cross[1] near the

[1] Newport's Relation.

Falls of James River, suitably inscribed, and took possession of the country in the name of Christ, and King James. The Maryland colonists claimed the region, between the Potomac and Atlantic, in March 1634, with similar ceremonies.

During the year 1635, the Jesuit Mission near Saint Mary, was composed of Father White, Altham alias Gravener, Thomas Gervase, and John Knowles, lay-assistant.[1] Like the Jesuits of Canada, engaging in trade and farming, as a means of support, they employed many servants.[2]

On the 11th of December, 1635, the Privy Council of England considered a charge, that Francis Rabnett of Maryland, a servant of a brother of Sir John Winter, had declared "that it" was lawful and meritorious

[1] In the catalogue of Clerkenwell College, 1627, in the Camden Society Publications are the following names:

Johannes Gravenerius.
Thomas Gervasii.
Philippus Fisherus [alias Musket].

[2] In the Annapolis Land Records there is the following list of servants of Mr. Andrew White and Altham for 1633–4:

Thos. Statham,	Robert Simpson,	Mary Jennings,
Matthias Sousa,	John Hilliard,	Robert Shirley,
M. Rogers,	John Hill,	Christopher Carnock,
John Bryant,	Wm. Ashmore,	Rich'd Lusthead,
Mich. Hervey,	Robt. Edwards,	Thos. Charinton,
Wm. Edwyn,	Thos. Grimston,	Rich'd Duke,
H'y Bishop,	Thos. Hatch,	John Thomson,
John Thornton,	Lewis Fremonds,	John Hollis,
Rich'd Cole,	John Elkin,	Thos. Hodges.
Rich'd Nevill or Nicholl,		

to kill a heretic king." Commissioner Hawley, who was present at the discussion, was asked if he had ever declared that "he was come to plant in Maryland the Romish religion." He "utterly denied" that he had ever made that statement.[1]

Before or during the year 1637, came Fathers Ferdinand Pulton,[2] Thomas Copley,[3] and lay-brother Walter Morley.

Copley was the grandson of Thomas Copley, who fled to Paris during Queen Elizabeth's reign, and was knighted by the King of France. His father, William, married Margaretta Prideaux, who had been educated under her aunt, a Prioress at Louvain. Among the records of the Province of Maryland, at Annapolis, is the following warrant of Charles the First.

"Whereas Thomas Copley gentleman, an alien born, is a recusant, and may be subject to be troubled for his religion, and forasmuch we are well satisfied of the conditions and qualities of the said Thomas Copley and of his loyalty and obedience towards us we do

---

[1] State Papers.

[2] On Nov. 30, 1638, applied for land due by conditions of plantation, for transporting

Walter Morley, Richard Disney, and Charles, the Welshman.

[3] On August 8, 1637, Mr. Thomas Copley and Mr. John Knolls transported.

Robert Kadger,	Luke Gardner,	Walter King,
Thos. Davison,	Thos. Motham,	George White,
Richard Cox,	John Martin,	John Tue.
Robert Sedgrave,	Jas. Compton,	

hereby will and require you, and every of you whom it may concern, to permit and further the said Thomas Copley freely and quietly to attend in any place, and to go about and follow his occupation, without molesting or troubling him, by any means whatsoever for matters of religion, or the persons and places of those unto whom he shall resort, and this shall be your warrant in his behalf.

"Give, under our signet, at our Palace at Westminster, the 10th day of December, in the 10th year of our reign."

Among the Land Office memoranda is the following: "Thomas Copley Esq., demandeth 4000 acres of land, due by conditions of plantations, for transporting into this Province himself and twenty able men, at his own charge to plant and inhabit, in the year 1637."

A few months later, it is recorded that there has been "shipped in the St. Margaret, for Thomas Copley Esq., cloth, hatchets, knives, hoes, to trade with the Indians for beaver.

On November 30th of this year, also came John Lewger the first Secretary of the Province, who had been a fellow student of Cecil, Lord Baltimore, at Oxford, and after graduation a clergyman of the Church of England. Becoming a member of the Church of Rome, he was made Secretary of the Colony and exercised great influence.[1] Soon after his arrival

[1] See page 69.

there was a revival of religion, which the Jesuit Relation of 1638 alludes to, in these words:

"Four fathers gave their attention to this Mission, with one assistant in temporal affairs; and he, indeed, after enduring severe toils for the space of five years, with the greatest patience, humility, and ardent love chanced to be seized by the disease prevailing at the time, and happily exchanged this wretched life, for an immortal one.

"He was also shortly followed by one of the Fathers, who was young indeed, but on account of his remarkable qualities of mind, evidently of great promise. He had scarcely spent two months in this mission, when to the great grief of all of us, he was carried off by the common sickness prevailing in the Colony, from which no one of the three preceding priests had escaped unharmed, yet we have not ceased to labor to the best of our ability among the neighboring people.

"And though the rulers of this Colony have not yet allowed us to dwell among the savages, both on account of the prevailing sickness and also because of the hostile disposition * * * * yet we hope that one of us will shortly secure a station among the barbarians.

"Meanwhile, we devote ourselves more zealously to the English, and since there are Protestants as well as Catholics in the Colony, we have labored for both and God has blessed our labors. For among the Protestants, nearly all who have come from England in this year,

1638, and many others have been converted to the faith, together with four servants, and five mechanics whom we hired for a month, and have in the meantime won to God * * * * * * * * * * * * * *

"The sick and the dying, who have been very numerous this year and who dwelt far apart we have assisted in every way so that not even a single one has died without the sacraments. We have buried very many and baptized various persons. And although there are not wanting frequent occasions of dissension, yet none of any importance has arisen here in the last nine months, which we have not immediately allayed."

It was in July of this year, that William Lewis[1] was fined for his contemptuous speeches concerning the clergy of the Church of England. Robert Sedgrave,[2] one of the servants transported by Father Copley, drew up the following complaint, to be signed by the freemen and then presented to the Governor and Council.

"This is to give you notice of the abuses and scandalous reproaches which God and his ministers do daily suffer by William Lewis of St. Marie's, who saith that our ministers, are ministers of the Divell, and that our books are made by the instruments of the Divell, and further saith, that those servants which are

---

[1] William Lewis in Nov., 1638, married Ursula Gifford. He was in the fight against the friends of Parliament in the spring of 1655 and executed for treason. His widow in 1657 married a George Guttridge.

[2] Sedgrave, Duke, and others hired by the Jesuits were Protestants.

under his charge shall not keep nor read any book which doth appertain to our religion, within the house of the said William Lewis, to the great discomfort of those poor bondmen which are under his subjection, especially in this heathen country, where no godly minister is to teach and instruct ignorant people in the grounds of religion. And as for people which cometh unto the said Lewis, or otherwise to pass the week, the said Lewis taketh occasion to call them into his chamber, and there laboureth with all vehemency, craft, and subtlety to delude ignorant persons.

"Therefore we beseech you, brethren in our Lord and Saviour Christ Jesus, that you who have power, that you will do in what lieth in you, to have these absurd abuses and the ridiculous crimes to be reclaimed, and that God and his ministers may not be so heinously trodden down by such ignominious speeches," etc.

It was in the year 1638, that the first Maryland Assembly met, whose proceedings have been preserved. The persons present, or voting by proxy, were ninety, of whom twelve were Roman Catholics, including the Jesuits White, Altham, and Copley. In 1639, the Jesuit Mission consisted of Father John Brock, alias Morgan, Superior, Philip Fisher, alias Musket, Thomas Copley[1] and John Gravener, and in a letter one of

[1] John Gee, in Foot out of the Snare, published in 1624, mentions Father Fisher alias Musket, and Copley and Poulton. He writes,

them states: "This year twelve heretics in all, wearied of former errors, have returned to favor with God and the Church."

Missions were begun among the Indians, and Father White visited Piscataway on the Potomac not many miles below Washington, where the Chief Tayac united with the Church of Rome. The Jesuit Relation states that the Chief had a wonderful vision:

"That his father, deceased some time before, appeared to be present before his eyes, accompanied by a god of a black color, whom he worshipped beseeching him that he would not desert him.

"At a short distance a most hideous demon, with a certain Snow, an obstinate heretic from England: and at length in another part the Governor of the Colony and Father White appeared, a god also being his companion, but much more beautiful, who excelled the unstained snow in whiteness, seeming gently to beckon the King to him. From that time he treated both the Governor and Father with the greatest affection."

Justinian Snow was one of the founders of Maryland,

"Father Musket a secular priest lodging over against St. Andrew's church, Holborn, a frequent preacher and one that hath much concourse of people to his chamber."

In Rushworth, vol. IV, pp. 44, 68, it is mentioned that Fisher for a time was in Newgate Prison, but by the influence of Secretary Windebank was released and harbored until he found an opportunity to go to America.

Gee alludes to "Father Copley Junior one that hath newly taken orders, and come from beyond seas."

and Lord Baltimore's factor in the Indian trade. A brother Abel was clerk in the Chancery Office, London, and Marmaduke, another, came afterwards to the Province, and both he and Justinian, in 1638, were members of the Assembly.

The latter died in 1639, and Marmaduke became administrator, but in consequence of sickness returned to England, and was living in 1659 in County Strafford, at Fenny Hill. In the absence of Marmaduke, Surgeon Thomas Gerrard, who married his sister Susanna, attended to the affairs of the brothers Snow.

On the 21st of August, 1638, Lord Baltimore relinquished the right to frame laws to be assented to by the Provincial Assembly, and granted to them the privilege of making their own laws, subject to his approval. Under this privilege, a legislature convened, on the 25th of February, 1639, and the first law enacted was, "that Holy Church shall have and enjoy all her rights, liberties, and franchises, wholly and without blemish."

This is the language of the English Statute Book, since the days of Henry the Second, who ratified Magna Charta. It was enacted, A.D. 1225, that: "The Church of England shall be free, and shall have all her rights and liabilities inviolable." Fifty years later, in the days of Edward the First, it was declared that "the peace of the Holy Church shall be kept and maintained in all points." A century later, in the reign of Edward the Third, the phraseology is, "Holy Church shall have all her liberties and franchises in quietness."

In A.D. 1377, at the commencement of the reign of Richard the Second, it was declared that, "Holy Church shall have and enjoy all her rights, liberties and franchises wholly and without blemish."

During the reign of Henry the Eighth, it was enacted by Parliament, that the King of England should be "Supreme Head on earth of the Church of England," any usage, custom, foreign laws, foreign authority, prescription, or any thing or things to the contrary notwithstanding. After this period, the Holy Church of the English Statute, was that Church, of which the King was the supreme head.

By the charter of Maryland, the ecclesiastical law of England, was made the law of the Province.[1]

In 1642 Father White and three other Jesuits were in Maryland. Father Philip Fisher, the Superior, was at Saint Mary, Roger Rigby on the Patuxent, and Andrew White at Piscataway, on the Potomac, nearly opposite Mount Vernon.

Notwithstanding there was no Church of England minister in the Province, the Snow family, and other Protestant Catholics, appear to have held religious

[1] Sir Edward Northey, Attorney General of England, gave this decision:

"As to the said clause in the grant of the province of Maryland, I am of opinion the same doth not give him power to do anything contrary to the ecclesiastical laws of England."—*Chalmers's Opinions.*

services. Surgeon Thomas Gerrard, whose wife and son-in-law were decided Protestant Catholics, had legal difficulties in 1642, relative to the use of a chapel, probably growing out of his position, as the acting administrator of the estate of Justinian Snow.

David Wickliff,[1] in March, 1642, complained to the Assembly, in behalf of the Protestant Catholics, that Gerrard had taken away the key of their chapel, and removed the books. The case was heard, and he was ordered to relinquish all title to the chapel, to restore the books, and pay a fine of five hundred pounds of tobacco, for the support of the first Protestant Catholic minister who should settle in the Province.

The news, that the only religious teachers in Maryland, were Jesuits, created great dissatisfaction in England, and the House of Commons, on December 1, 1641, presented an address to Charles the First, at Hampton Court, in which they complained that he had permitted "another State moulded within this State, independent in government, contrary in interest and affection, secretly corrupting the ignorant or negligent professors of religion."[2] Lord Baltimore perceived that loyal English subjects would continue to shun Maryland, if he continued to favor the Jesuits, and his poverty was so great, that unless he received a revenue from his Province, he must continue to depend

[1] Wickliff in 1638 was entered as one of the servants of George Evelyn.

[2] Rushworth, vol. IV.

upon his father-in-law, Earl Arundel, for bread to support his family. Determining to attract Protestant colonists, he offended the Jesuits. Without his consent, they had received a present of land from the converted Piscataway Chief, and he therefore sent over certain instructions, for the obtaining of land.

When Governor Calvert and Secretary Lewger submitted these papers to the Jesuits, they objected.

A memorandum still preserved and supposed to be in the handwriting of John Lewger says:

"The Governor and I went to the good men about difficulties.

"1. About putting the statute of mortmain on all lands. Gov. Calvert construed it, so as that no man could have an additional grant, except he would accept the statute, for all his land.

"2. One of the good men thought that publishing the conditions of Plantation would not incur excommunication, but thought it might be a mortal sin, to propose an act or obligations against good manners or piety, or to assent to it.

"3. The oath in the instructions to be tendered to such as were to take land, was decided to be against conscience, and to incur excommunication *bullæ cœnæ*[1] to publish or administer any such oath."

[1] The Pope's Bull "In cœna Domini" was read every year on the day of the Lord's Supper or Maundy Thursday, and contained excommunications and anathemas against heretics and all who disturbed or opposed the jurisdiction of the Holy See.

The Governor and Lewger shrank from obeying Lord Baltimore, as they not did wish to be excommunicated from the Church of Rome. In September, 1642, two Jesuits in England desired to join the Maryland Mission, but Baltimore said, that he "could not in prudence allow them to go, unless an agreement was first made." On the 5th of October Lord Baltimore's sister wrote: "I have been with my brother, but he is inexorable until all conditions be agreed upon between you."

A few days after, the Jesuits assented to the following positions of the Proprietary.

"Considering the dependence of the Government of Maryland on the state of England, unto which it must, as near as may be, be comformable, no ecclesiastical person whatever inhabiting or being within the said Province ought to pretend or expect, nor is Lord Baltimore or any of his officers, although they be Roman Catholics, obliged in conscience to allow said ecclesiastics, in said Province, any more or other privileges, exemptions or immunities for their persons, lands or goods, than is allowed by his Majesty or his officers and magistrates to like persons in England."

"And any magistrates may proceed against the person, goods, etc., of such ecclesiastic for the doing of right and justice to another, or for maintaining his Proprietary prerogatives, and jurisdictions, just as against any other person, residing in said Province.

"These things to be done, without incurring the censure of *bullæ cœnæ*, or committing a sin for so doing.[1]

The Priests did not keep faith with Lord Baltimore, as we discover from the Jesuit Relation of this period. It says: "When our people declared it to be repugnant to the laws of the Church, two priests were sent from England, who might teach the contrary, but the reverse of what was expected, happened; for our reasons being heard, and the thing itself being more clearly understood, they easily fell in with our opinion."

The civil war in England growing out of resistance of the Parliament to the arbitrary demands of the King, induced strife in Maryland.

Under a letter of marque granted by Charles the First to Governor Calvert, he seized the ship of Capt. Richard Ingle of London in 1643. Ingle in retaliation obtained a commission from Parliament, and appeared with the ship Reformation, and attacked those who would not acknowledge the "Keepers of the liberties of England" as Parliament was styled.

During his stay Father Copley's house at Potopaco was attacked as well as the Jesuit plantation of St. Jingo. Fathers White and Fisher were taken prisoners, and brought to London. White was tried and found guilty of teaching doctrines contrary to the laws of England, but on the 4th of July, 1646, judg-

[1] Streeter's Early Maryland Papers.

ment was stayed. After remaining in Newgate prison for many months, in January 7, 1648, the House of Commons " did concur with the Lords in granting the petition of Andrew White, a Jesuit, who was brought out of America, into the kingdom, by force, upon an English ship," and he was ordered to be discharged provided he left the kingdom, within fifteen days.[1] He never returned to America, but Father Fisher appears to have resumed labor in 1649, with one companion, probably Father Lawrence Starkey who came at this time to Maryland. A letter of Fisher is extant addressed to his Superior in which he writes under date of March 1, 1648–9:

" Although my companion and myself reached Virginia on the 7th of January, after a tolerable journey of seven weeks, there I left my companion, and availed myself of the opportunity of proceeding to Maryland, where I arrived in the course of February."

During the uprising of the friends of Parliament under Ingle, Father Copley seems to have remained at St. Inigo. In a relation, appended to Father White's journal, there is narrated a very wonderful and indelicate story which proves that the Jesuit mission was not entirely broken up. It is in these words:

" It has been established by custom and usage of the Catholics who live in Maryland during the whole night of the 31st of July, following the festival of St. Ignatius,

[1] House of Common's Journal.

to honor with a salute of cannon, their tutelar guardian and patron saint.

"Wherefore in the year 1646, mindful of the solemn custom, the anniversary of the holy father being ended, they wished the night also consecrated to the honor of the same, by the continual discharge of artillery. At this time there were in the neighborhood certain soldiers, unjust plunderers, Englishmen indeed by birth, of the heterodox faith, who, coming the year before with a fleet had invaded with arms almost the entire colony, had plundered, burnt, and finally having abducted the priests and driven the Governor himself into exile, had reduced it to a miserable servitude. These had protection in a certain fortified citadel, built for their own defence, situated about five miles from the others; but now aroused by the nocturnal report of the cannon, the day after, that is, on the first of August, rush upon us with arms, break into the houses of the Catholics, and plunder whatever there is of arms or powder.

"After a while, when at length they had made an end of plundering, and had arranged their departure, one of them, a fellow of a beastly disposition and a scoffer both contemptible and blasphemous who dared to assail St. Ignatius himself with filthy scurrility and a more filthy act.

'"Away to the wicked cross with you, Papists,' says

he 'who take delight in saluting your poor saint, by the firing of cannon, I have a cannon too, and I will give him a salute more suitable and appropriate to so miserable a saint.'

"This being said (let me not offend the delicacy of your ears) he resounded with a loud report, and departed, while his companions deride with their insolent laughter.

"But his impious and wicked scurrility cost the wretch dear; for, scarcely had he proceeded two hundred paces from the place, when he felt a commotion of the bowels within, and that he was solicited to privacy; and when he had gone about the same distance on his way, he had to withdraw privately again, complaining of an unusual pain of his bowels, the like of which he had never felt in his life before. The remaining part of his journey; to wit: four miles, was accomplished in a boat, in which space, the severe torture of his bowels and the looseness of his belly frequently compelled him to land. Having arrived at the Fort, scarcely in possession of his mind, through so great pain, he rolls himself at one time on the ground, at another casts himself on a bench, again on a bed, crying out all the time with a loud voice 'I am burning up! I am burning up! There is a fire in my belly! There is a fire in my bowels!'

"The officers, having pitied the deplorable fate of their comrade, carry him at length, placed in a boat to a certain Thomas Hebden a skilful surgeon,[1] but the malady had proceeded further than could be cured or alleviated by his art. In the meantime you could hear nothing else coming from his lips, but that well known and mournful cry 'I am burning up! I am burning up! Fire! Fire!'

"The day after, which was the 2d of August, his intolerable suffering growing worse every hour, his bowels began to be voided, piecemeal. But on the 3d of August, furious and raging, he passed larger portions of the intestines some of which were a foot, some a foot and a half, others two feet long. At length the fourth day drained the whole pump, so that it left nothing remaining but the abdomen empty and void. Still surviving, he saw the dawning of the fifth day, when the unhappy wretch ceased to see and live, an example to posterity of divine vengeance warning mankind.

"Discite justitiam, moniti et non contemnere divos.' Innumerable persons still living, saw the intestines of the dead man for many months hang upon the fence posts; among whom was he who has added his testimony to these things, and with his hands handled the bowels, blackened, and as if crisped up, by this fire, of modern Judas."

---

[1] Thomas Hebden was in the employ of George Evelyn of Evelynton Manor at Piney Point in 1638, and a member of the Assembly. Streeter says he was a carpenter. In his will he requested Father Copley to pray for his soul.

RELIGIOUS CONDITION DURING THE ASCENDENCY OF PARLIAMENT.

LORD Baltimore, finding that few colonists would go to Maryland from England, undeterred by the threat of excommunication, appealed to Massachusetts through Major Edward Gibbons, described in an old chronicle as the "younger brother of the house of an honorable extraction,"[1] the owner of a windmill at St. Mary, a trader in the Potomac, and a prominent citizen of Boston. Gibbons once lost a vessel in the waters of Virginia and Maryland, and perhaps the Jesuits' letter of 1642 alludes to him in these words: "Father White suffered no little inconvenience from a hard-hearted and troublesome captain of New England, whom he had engaged for the purpose of taking him and his effects, from whom he was in fear a little while after, not without cause, that he would be either cast into the sea, or be carried with his property to New England, which is full of Puritan Calvinists, that is of all Calvinist heresy.

"Silently committing the thing to God, at length in

[1] Scottow.

safety reached Potomac, they vulgarly call it Patemeak, in which harbor, when they had cast anchor, the ship stuck so fast, bound by a great quantity of ice, that for the space of seventeen days, it could not be moved. Walking on the ice, as if on land, the Father departed for the town; and when the ice was broken up, the ship driven and jammed by the force and violence of the ice, sunk, the cargo being in a great measure recovered."

The year after the Jesuits refused to yield to the Proprietary, on the 13th of October, 1643, Governor Winthrop of Massachusetts makes the following entry in his Journal:

"The Lord Baltimore being owner of much land near Virginia, being himself a Papist and his brother Mr. Calvert, the Governor there a Papist also, but the colony consisting of both Protestant and Papist, he wrote a letter to Capt. Gibbons of Boston and sent him a commission wherein he made a tender of land in Maryland to any of ours that would transport themselves thither with free liberty of religion, and all other privileges which the place affords, paying such annual rent as should be agreed upon, but our Captain had no mind to further his desire, nor had any of our people temptation that way."

By an unexpected Providence, settlers at last came from Virginia, and the fortunes of Lord Baltimore by their advent were greatly improved. The Puritans of

Nansemond County, Virginia, in 1643 had secured the services of Rev. William Tompson a graduate of Oxford, John Knowles of Immanuel College, Cambridge, and Thomas James for their parishes. They were coldly received by Governor Berkeley, and his chaplain Thomas Harrison, because they were non-conformists. One month before the great massacre by the Indians, Berkeley secured the passage of an act forbidding any to officiate in churches who did not use the Book of Common Prayer. In a little while, the three ministers retired, but soon the Governor of Virginia was surprised by his able chaplain, Harrison, becoming a non-conformist, leaving Jamestown, and preaching to the Puritans of Nansemond and Elizabeth River.[1]

In 1644, Roger Williams of Rhode Island visited England and published a treatise on religious toleration, of which, a Chaplain of the Archbishop of Canterbury wrote: "Witness the book printed, 1644, called *The Bloody Tenet*, which the author affirmeth he wrote in milk; and if he did so, he hath put much rats-bane into it, as namely: That it is the will and command of God that since the coming of his Son, the Lord Jesus, a permission of the most Paganish, Jewish, Turkish or Anti-Christian consciences, and worships, be granted to all men in all nations and countries; that Civil States with their officers of justice, are not Go-

[1] Calamy and Winthrop.

vernors or defenders of the spiritual and Christian state and worship."[1]

At the same period, it was urged by the friends of Roger Williams "that the Parliament will provide that particular and private congregations may have public protection; that all statutes against the Separatists be reviewed and repealed; that the Press may be free for any man that writes nothing scandalous or dangerous to the State; that this Parliament prove themselves loving fathers to all sorts of good men, bearing respect unto all, and so inviting an equal assistance and affection from all."

On October 27th, 1645, the House of Commons ordered: "That the inhabitants of the Summer Islands, and such others as shall join themselves to them, shall, without any molestation or trouble, have and enjoy the liberty of the conscience, in matters of God's worship, as well in those parts of America, where they are now planted, as in all other parts of America where they may hereafter plant."[2]

The Rev. Patrick Copland,[3] Governor Sayle and

---

[1] Featley's *Dipper dipped.*

[2] Journal of House of Commons.

[3] Patrick Copland was an earnest and useful clergyman of whom too little has been known. In 1614 he was Chaplain of one of the ships of the East India Company. In 1616 returned to England accompanied by a talented native youth whom he had taught chiefly by signs, "to speak, to read, and write the English tongue, both Roman and Secretary, within less than the space of a year." At his suggestion the lad was publicly baptized on Dec. 22, 1616, in St. Dennis church, London, "as the first fruits of India."

others for conscience sake left the Somers Islands, and settled at Eleuthera, a small isle of the Bahamas group, adjoining Guanahani or Cat Island, the first land of the West, seen by Columbus. Sayle visited the Puritans of Virginia, and invited them to go to the Patmos, which their fellow religionists had selected, but they declined.

The Rev. Thomas Harrison, in a letter dated November 2, 1646, and sent to Governor Winthrop of Massachusetts, by Capt. Edward Gibbons, afterwards appointed Admiral of Maryland, writes: "Had your proposition found us risen up, in a posture of removal, there is weight and force enough [in yours] to have staked us down again."

Not long after, in 1617, Copland with his pupil, sailed for the Indian Ocean in the Royal James, one of the fleet which Sir Thomas Dale, late Governor of Virginia, assumed the command of on Sept. 19, 1618. In the presence of Dale, in view of an impending naval conflict with the Dutch on the 2d of December, Copland preached on the Royal James. On the 9th of August, 1619, Dale died, and his old associate Sir Thomas Gates died in the same service the next year.

On the 26th of April, 1620, Copland in the Royal James went to Japan.

Leaving Java in February, 1621, the ship slowly returned to England, and having become interested in Virginia by conversing with Dale and Gates, on the homeward voyage he collected from fellow passengers, £70, for a church or school in Virginia.

Arriving in the Thames about the middle of September, the next month John Ferrar, Deputy Governor of Virginia Company, announced the collection, to the members. The next year Copland preached before the Company, and the sermon was published with the following title:

Virginia's God be thanked | or | a Sermon of | Thanksgiuing | for

The steady persistence of Harrison, and the increase of his congregations, irritated Governor Berkeley, and

---

the happie | Successe of the affayres in | Virginia this last | yeare | preached by Patrick Copland at | *Bow*-Church, in *Cheapside*, before the Honorable | Virginia Company, on Thursday, the 18 | of *Aprill* 1622. And now published by | *the Commandement of the said hono* | *rable* Company. | Hereunto are adjoyned some Epistles, | written first in Latine (and now Englished) in the East Indies by *Peter Pope*, an Indian youth, | *borne in the Bay of Bengale*, who was first taught | and converted by the said P. C. And after bap- | tized by Master *John Wood*, Dr. in Divinitie | *in a famous Assembly, before the Right* | *Worshipfull, the East India Company*, | at S. *Denis* in Fan-Church Streete | in *London*, December 22, | 1616 | London | Printed by J. D. for *William Sheffard* and John Bellamie, and are to be sold at his shop, at the two Grey- | hounds in Corne-hill, neere the Royall | *Exchange* 1622. |

In this sermon is an allusion to the motto of the Seal of the Virginia Company, which was the motto of the Colony until the Revolution of 1776. He speaks of "This noble Plantation tending so highly to the advancement of the Gospel, and to the honoring of our dread Sovereign, by inlarging of his kingdoms, and adding a fifth crown unto his other four; for 'En dat Virginia quintam,' is the motto of the legal seal of Virginia."

On October 20, 1619, the Company appointed a Committee to meet at Sir Edwin Sandys', "to take a cote for Virginia, and agree upon the Seale." On the 15th of the next month the device was presented for inspection. When the seal was presented to King James, he looked at the reverse with the figure of St. George slaying the Dragon, with the motto, "Fas alium superare draconem," referring to the heathenism of the Indians, and ordered that the motto should not be used.

The face of the legal seal was an escutcheon, quartered with the arms of England, France, Scotland, and Ireland; crested with a maiden Queen, with flowing hair and eastern crown; supporters, two men in armor.

in the face of the action of Parliament, he influenced the Assembly of Virginia, on the 3d of November, 1647, to enact the following:

"Upon divers informations presented to this Assem-

Spenser, Sir Walter Raleigh's friend, dedicated his *Fairy Queen* to Elizabeth "Queen of England, France, Ireland, and Virginia." After James of Scotland became King of England, Virginia could be called, in compliment, the fifth kingdom.

In the "Mask of Flowers," played by the Gentlemen of Gray's Inn upon 12th night, 1613–14 in honor of the nuptials of Somerset, Kawasha, a God of the Virginians appears, and in the play occurs the following:

"But now is Britannie fit to be
A seat for a fifth Monarchie.

Copland was elected Rector of the College at Henrico, but the massacre by the Indians in the spring of 1622 thwarted his design of residing in Virginia.

John Ferrar's brother Nicholas, who became a clergyman, sympathized with Copland in the desire to educate the Indian children of North America, and aided in establishing a school at the Somers Islands. When he became a non-conformist is unknown.

In December, 1638, the celebrated divine Hugh Peters, then of Salem, Mass., writes a letter "To my worthy and reverend Brother, Mr. Copeland, Minister of the Gospel in Bermudas."

While residing in Pagets' tribe, Copland gave a tract of land for a free school. In a letter from this settlement, dated 4th of December, 1639, and addressed to Governor Winthrop of Boston, he thanks him for twelve New England Indians sent to be educated, but were left at Providence island. He adds: "If they had safely arrived here, I would have had a care of them to have disposed of them to such honest men, as should have trained them up in the principles of religion, and so when they had been fit for your plantation, have returned them again to have done God some service, in being instruments to do some good for their country."

He then tells Winthrop how the Dutch at Amboyna, East Indies, copied the Jesuit method of training and educated their own children and the native youth in the same school, each acquiring the other's language. He continues: "Being at Naugasack, a famous city of Japan, I saw with my own eyes, monuments of many fair churches

bly against several ministers for their neglect and refractory refusing, after warning given to them, to read Common Prayer in Divine service upon the Sabbath days, contrary to the canons of the Church, and the Acts of Parliament therein established: for future remedy hereof,

"Be it enacted, by Governor, Council and Burgesses of this Grand Assembly, That all ministers in their

---

and a University which sometimes they had there, but by their pragmatic intermeddling with State matters was banished from Japan." He then stated that he had "a Papist catechism in my study, imprinted at Naugasack, with the Italian letters, in Japan tongue."

The letter concludes by recommending for education George Stirke, the son of a lately deceased scholar, poet, and minister of the Islands. Young Stirke entered Cambridge, graduated in 1641, and became a man of science.

Although the House of Commons in 1645, had ordered liberty of conscience and worship in the Plantations, the Independents of Somers Island and Virginia were oppressed by those in power.

In behalf of the Congregationalists of the former place, Captain Sayle explored and selected one of the isles of the Bahamas, for the use of all who desire entire freedom of worship. He then went to Virginia and extended an invitation to Rev. Mr. Harrison's congregation to cast in their lot with them. In November, 1646, he and the Rev. Mr. Golding came to Boston and from thence sailed to England, where they obtained a patent from Parliament, for the settling of Eleuthera, with provision for entire liberty of conscience. Upon Sayle's return, about seventy persons left Somers Island for Eleuthera, among whom was the venerable Patrick Copland nearly eighty years of age. The isle proved a dreary place, and they suffered for food. The Boston churches hearing of their destitution in 1650 or 1651, sent to them a ship filled with supplies, which arrived on Sunday, just as their faithful pastor had finished an exposition of the 23d Psalm.

Authorities consulted in preparing of the above sketch: *Calendar of East India Co. Papers; Virginia Co. MSS.; Hubbard, Winslow, Johnson, Winthrop, Nichols Progresses of King James.*

several cures throughout the Colony do duly, upon every Sabbath day, read such prayers as are appointed and prescribed unto them, by the said Book of Common Prayer.

"And be it further enacted, as a further penalty to such as have neglected, or shall neglect their duty herein, that no parishioners shall be compelled, either by distress or otherwise, to pay any manner of tithes or duties, to any non-conformist aforesaid."

The next year Berkeley ordered Harrison, and Elder William Durand to leave Virginia.[1] Harrison went

[1] William Durand of Upper Norfolk in Virginia had listened to the preaching of Rev. John Davenport, first minister of New Haven, Ct., when he was Vicar of St. Stephens, Coleman street, London.

There came with him to Maryland in 1648, his wife, his daughter Elizabeth, and four other children. Two freemen, William Pell and —— Archer, and servants *Thomas Marsh*, Margaret Marsh, William Warren, William Hogg, and Ann Coles. The Commissioners who in 1652, made a treaty with the Susquehannas, at the Severn River were Richard Bennett, Edward Lloyd, William Fuller, Leonard Strong and *Thomas Marsh.*

In October 1651, Durand obtained a grant of land at the Cliffs of the Chespeake in Calvert County, near the possessions of Leonard Strong and William Fuller. In 1654, he was made Secretary of the Province. When the Quakers arrived he was kind to them, and one of the Society of Friends in 1658, writes "William Fuller abides unmoved: I know not but that William Durand doth the like."

Rev. Thomas Harrison received the degree of D.D., after he went to England. On October 11th, 1649, the Council of State wrote to Governor Berkeley that they were informed, by petition of the congregation of Nansemond, that their minister Mr. Harrison, an able man, of unblamable conversation had been banished the Colony because he would not conform to the use of the Common Prayer Book, and as he could not be ignorant, that the use of it was prohibited by Parliament, he was directed to allow Mr. Harrison to return to his ministry."

to Boston, consulted with friends, and as a result sailed for England, to complain of Berkeley's tyranny, and Durand began to negotiate for a settlement in Maryland.

Upon the express assurance, that there would be a modification of the oaths of office and fidelity, an enjoyment of liberty of conscience, and the privilege of choice in officers, the Virginia non-conformists agreed to remove to the banks of the Severn.[1]

Harrison never went back but became Chaplain of Cromwell's son Henry, when Lord Lieutenant of Ireland. He was in Dublin at the time of Oliver Cromwell's death, and preached a funeral sermon from Lamentations 5 ch. 16 v. "The crown is fallen from our head; wo unto us that we have sinned." It was published with the following title: "Threni Hybernici: or Ireland sympathizing with England and Scotland, in a sad lamentation for the loss of their Josiah. Represented in a sermon at Christ Church in Dublin, before his Excellency the Lord Deputy, with divers of the Nobility, Gentry, and Commonality there assembled to celebrate a funeral solemnity, upon the death of the Lord Protector; by Dr. Harrison, Chief Chaplain to his said Excellency."

Upon the accession of Charles the Second, unable to accept the terms of conformity, he retired to Chester, England. An officer on the 3d of July, 1665, reports: "A conventicle of one hundred persons was appointed at the house of Dr. Thomas Harrison, late Chaplain of Harry Cromwell; broke open the house, found some under the beds, others in the closets, and thirty were taken before the Mayor."

Just before he left America, he married Dorothy, daughter of Samuel Symonds formerly of Yeldham, Essex, who came to Ipswich, Mass., in 1637 and died in 1678, having been for several years Deputy Governor, and respected for his great worth. Mrs. Lucy Downing, sister of Gov. Winthrop, of Mass., in a letter to her nephew, John Winthrop of Ct., writes under date of Dec. 17, 1648. "You hear, I believe, our cousin Dorothy Simonds, is now won and wedded to Mr. Harrison, the Virginia minister."

[1] Hammond.

William Stone of Hungar's Neck, Eastern Shore of Virginia, a nephew of Thomas Stone, haberdasher of London, and brother-in-law of Francis Doughty,[1] a non-conformist minister, was on the 6th of August, 1648, commissioned Governor, in the place of Thomas Green.

In accordance with stipulations with the Puritans, in his commission, is found for the first time, the pledge, not to disturb any person professing to believe in Jesus Christ merely for, or in respect of his or her religion, or the free exercise thereof.[2]

---

[1] In Governor Stone's will Francis Doughty is called his brother-in-law. Donghty was the son of a Bristol alderman and probably the same person who when Vicar of Sodbury, Gloucester, had been arraigned before the High Commissioner, for contempt of his Sacred Majesty, having spoken of him, in prayer, as "Charles by common election, and general consent, King of England."

In 1639, he came to Massachusetts, and from thence went to Long Island, and while there used to preach to the English-speaking members of the Reformed Church in Manhattan, now New York City. His daughter Mary, there married Adrian Vander Donk, a Leyden graduate and distinguished lawyer. After his decease, she became the wife of Hugh O'Neal of Patuxent, Maryland, and her father appears to have resided in the same vicinity. Herrman, one of the New Netherlands Commissioners, says that while he was dining with Philip Calvert, on Sunday, the 12th of October, 1659, "Mr. Doughty, the minister accidentally called."

[2] Streeter who made a thorough investigation says: "Mr. Chalmers was in error, when he asserted, that in the oath taken by the Governor and Council, *between* the years 1637 and 1657, there was a clause binding them not to molest any one, on account of his religion, who professed to believe in Jesus Christ. The oath of 1639 is the first on record administered to the Governor and Council; and it most carefully avoids all allusion to religion. The same form was certainly in use, as late as April, 1643, when James Neal took the oath of Councillor,

Plowden, who had lived in Virginia, at the time of the controversy, between Berkeley and the non-conformists, in the description of *Nova Albion*, published in London, 1648, advocated the principle, insisted upon by the Puritans, as a condition of residence in Maryland. He writes of religion in these words: "I conceive the Holland way, now practiced, best to content all parties. By Act of Parliament or General Assembly to settle and establish all the fundamentals necessary to salvation, as the three creeds, the commandments, preaching on the Lord's Day, and great days, and catechism in the afternoon, the sacraments of the altar and baptism

"But no persecution to any dissenting, and to all such, as to the Walloons, free chapels, and to punish all as seditious and for contempt, as bitter, rail, and condemn others of the contrary; for this argument or persuasion, all religious ceremonies or church discipline should be acted in mildness, love, and charity, and gentle language, not to disturb the peace or quietness of the inhabitants."

---

as is distinctly stated, according to the form described in the act of Assembly of March, 1639.

If Chalmers meant by the expression "between 1637," for 1637, as many have contended, he was clearly mistaken; if he intended to leave the date unfixed, he has given himself large scope, and afforded ground for false inferences.

The prohibition in regard to molesting believers in Christ cannot be found in any commission before that to Governor Stone in August, 1648. Streeter's *Early Papers;* M'd Hist. Soc. Publication, 1876, pp. 243, 244.

The legislature of 1649 embodied the agreement, and the principie recognized in Stone's commission, in the " Act concerning Religion."

Hammond, a friend of Lord Baltimore, but hostile to the non-conformists, asserts, that the inhabitants were composed of conformists, non-conformists, and a " few Papists."

In a pamphlet published at London, in 1656, he writes: " And there was in Virginia, a certain people congregated into a church, calling themselves Independents, which daily increasing, several consultations were held by the State of that Colony, how to suppress them, which was duly put in execution, as first, the pastor was banished, next other teachers, then many by informations clapt up in prsion, then generally disarmed, which was very harsh. * * * * * * * *

" Maryland was counted by them as a refuge, the Lord Proprietor and his Governor solicited, and several addresses made for their admittance and entertainment into that Province." These conditions were presented; "that they should have convenient portion of land assigned, the liberty of conscience, and privilege to choose their own officers." He continues, " An Assembly was called throughout the whole country, after their coming over, consisting as well of themselves, as the rest, and because there were some few Papists that first inhabited, these themselves, and others, being of different judgments, an Act was passed that all professing in Jesus Christ should have equal justice."[1] Hammond further states, that at the request of the Virginia Puritans, "the oath of fidelity was overhauled, and this clause added to it, 'provided it infringe not the liberty of conscience.'"

The Act was not approved by Lord Baltimore for many months. In the Record Book, the following note is appended, signed Philip Calvert. "An Act of Assembly, 21st April, 1649, confirmed by the Lord Proprietary by an instrument under his hand and seal dated Aug. 26, 1650."[2]

Lord Baltimore's defence before Parliament, speaks of this law originating in Maryland. He writes in one place: "Although those laws were assented unto by the Lord Baltimore in August, 1650, yet it appears, that some of them were enacted in Maryland, by the Assembly there, in April 1649." In another place, speaking of a law of 1650, is the following statement:

"It was one of those laws passed by the Assembly in Maryland, in April 1650, when the people there knew of the late King's death, a year after, the other law above mentioned, with divers others, which were enacted in April, 1649,[3] as aforesaid, though in the in-

[1] *Leah and Rachel.* London, 1656.

[2] Annapolis Manuscripts.

[3] Blome in his *Britannia* published in 1673, at London, and to which book Cecil, Lord Baltimore was a subscriber, asserts that "His Lordship, by advice of the General Assembly of the province, hath long since established a model of good and wholesome laws, with toleration of religion, to all sorts, that profess faith in Christ."

grossment of them all here, when the Lord Baltimore gave his assent to them altogether, in August 1650, it was written before it, because they were transposed here, in such order, as the Lord Baltimore thought fit, according to the nature, and more or less importance of them, placing the Act concerning Religion first."[1]

This Act was contrary to the teachings of the Church of Rome, since it was the recognition of Christians who rejected the Pope, and when the Assembly of 1650 met, there was an expression of dissatisfaction.

The burgesses of the Assembly were as follows.

John Hatch,	St. George's Hundred.
Walter Beane,	" " "
John Medley,	Newtown "
William Brough,	" "
Robert Robins,	" "
Francis Posey,	St. Clement's "
Philip Land,	St. Mary's "
Francis Brooks,	" " "
Thomas Mathews,	St. Inigo's "
Thomas Sterman,	St. Michael's "
George Manners,	" " "
James Cox,	Anne Arundel
George Puddington,	" " "

When the delegates came to be sworn, all the Roman Catholics, four in number, objected to the principles of the Act concerning Religion, passed by the last

[1] *The Lord Baltimore's Case.* London, 1653.

Assembly. Medley, Manners, and Land thought it was not right to have a perpetual law upon the subject, but Thomas Mathews, who came from the precinct in which the home of the Jesuits was situated, told the Assembly, that he could not take the oath of toleration, "as he wished to be guided, in matters of conscience, by spiritual counsel."[1]

He was then censured and expelled, and Cuthbert Fenwick was returned in his place.

It was not, until after the Act concerning Religion, was passed, that any Protestant clergyman permanently settled in the Province.

About the year 1650, there arrived William Wilkinson, Cl'k, about fifty years of age, with his wife, daughters Mary, Rebecca, Elizabeth, step-daughter Margaret, and servants Robert Cornish, and Ann Stevens. Like Father Thomas Copley, he engaged in trade, to assist in his support.[2]

---

[1] Annapolis Manuscripts.

[2] Early in 1654 Stringer, a carpenter, died at Wilkinson's house, and left chests, locked up in the store. In rendering the account of this man's estate, the Minister presents a curious mingling of charges, in tobacco weight.

For the use of his boat and a boy.	lbs. 50
" boarding at his house 7 or 8 days and 2 men.	400
" funeral sermon.	100
" " dinner.	300
" a plank for his coffin.	60

In his will made May 29, 1663, his daughter Rebecca is spoken of as the wife of William Hatton, and Eliza as the wife of Thomas Dent.

Dent was among the first settlers in the District of Columbia.

In 1662 he entered a tract of land called Gisborough, on the east side of Anacostan River, in a branch called Eastern Branch. The name

In 1652 Captain William Mitchell, one of the worst men in the Province, was appointed a member of the Council, by Lord Baltimore. He was suspected of poisoning his wife on a voyage to America. Ann, daughter of Elizabeth Bolton, of St. Martins in the Fields, Middlesex, was hired as a servant, to act as governess, whom he harshly used, and then sold to Francis Brooke, for a wife.

At a Court, held on 22d of June, 1652, at Saint Mary's, Thomas Cole, aged thirty-two years, deposed: "That before coming out of England he was at Mr. Edmond Plowden's chamber. He asked me with whom I lived? I replied Capt. Mitchell. He persuading me not to go with him to Virginia, asked me 'Of what religion he was, and whether I ever saw him go to church?' I made answer 'I never saw him go to church.' He replied, 'that Captain Mitchell being among a company of gentlemen, he wondered, that the world had been, so many hundred years, deluded with a man and a pigeon.'"

Mr. Plowden then told Cole, that by the dove, was meant "the Holy Ghost," and by the man, "our Saviour, Christ."

The Province of Maryland, in 1652, by commission-

is still retained, and the U. S. Government Asylum for the Insane is on or near the tract.

The place was probably called from Gisborough a town on the flats of the river Tees in North Yorkshire, where a Dent family lived.

In 1672 Rev. Mr. Nicholet of Salem, Mass., who had lived in Maryland, spoke of five Protestants whom he often met, Mr. Dent, Mr. Hatton, Mr. Hill, Mr. Hanson, and Mr. Thoroughgood.

ers from Parliament, was reduced and settled with the authority of the Commonwealth of England, and Governor Stone was continued in office, having promised to issue all writs and other processes in the name of "the keepers of the liberty of England."

The next year, under directions from Lord Baltimore, Stone violated the compact, and began to issue writs in the Lord Proprietary's name, to admit to the Council only those appointed by Lord Baltimore, and require the inhabitants to take an oath of fidelity, which if refused by any colonist, after three months his lands were to be confiscated for the use of the Proprietary.

At the request of Richard Preston, and over one hundred other planters, the Parliament Commissioners visited Maryland, and on the 20th of July, 1654, Stone "laid down his power as Governor of this province under his Lordship, and did promise for the future to submit to such government as shall be selected by the Commissioners, in the name and under the authority of His Highness, the Lord Protector."

In 1653 Lord Baltimore printed the statement of his reasons, as presented to Parliament, why his charter should not be abrogated. The last is as follows: "If the Lord Baltimore should by this Commonwealth, be prejudiced in any of the rights or privileges of his patent of that Province; it would be a great discouragement, to others in foreign plantations, upon any exigency to adhere to the interest of this Commonwealth; because it is notoriously known, that by his express direction, his officers and the people there did adhere to the interest of this Commonwealth, when all other English plantations, except New England, declared against the Parliament, and at that time received their friends, in time of distress, for which, he was like, divers times, to be deprived of his interest there, by the colony of Virginia, and others, who had commissions from the late King's eldest son, for that purpose, as appears by a commission, granted by him to Sir Wm. Davenant."[1]

In this pamphlet he also states that his opponents in Maryland were "obscure and factious fellows."

---

[1] Sir Wm. Davenant K't was Shakspeare's godson, and like his godfather was given to poetry. On the 16th day of February, 1649–50, Charles issued a commission from his exile in Jersey, the opening paragraphs of which were as follows:

"Whereas the Lord Baltimore, Proprietary of the Province and plantations in Maryland, in America doth visibly adhere to the rebels of England, and admit all kinds of schismatics and sectaries, and other ill affected persons, with the said plantations of Maryland, so that we have cause to apprehend very great prejudice to our service thereby, and very great danger to our plantations in Virginia, who have carried themselves, with so much loyalty and fidelity to the King, our Father of blessed memory, and to us, Know ye, therefore, that we reposing special trust and confidence in the courage, conduct, loyalty, and good affection of Sir Wm. Davenant, and for prevention of the danger and inconveniences above mentioned, do by these presents, nominate, constitute, and appoint you, our Lieutenant Governor of the said province or plantations of Maryland."

With the aid of Queen Henrietta Maria, Davenant sailed from a port in Normandy, with a company of weavers and mechanics, but on the voyage, was captured, and brought to England. Lodged in the Tower, he there finished his poem of Gondibert, and at length was released "from durance vile," by the intercession of the great Puritan poet, John Milton.

A review of this publication was in 1655, printed in London, which thus answers this allusion.

"The Lord Baltimore pretends, in print, his entertainment in Maryland, of the Parliament friends thrust out of Virginia; but those very men whom he so styles, coming thither, being promised by Captain Stone, he would decline urging the oath upon them, complain of it, to the Parliament, are in answer there unto vilified by Lord Baltimore, and publicly taxed for obscure and factious fellows; and in his later letters, termed the basest of men, and unworthy of the least favor or forbearance.

"Such advantages doth he make on all sides, at such a distance, and in such uncomposed times, that he confidently takes the liberty, to aver such extreme and contrary things, which amaze other men, that see them. The place as himself confessed, had been deserted, if not peopled from Virginia."

In 1652, Father Thomas Copley died, and Father Lawrence Starkey assumed the duties he performed. Starkey was born in Lancashire in 1606, and at the age of thirty joined the order of Jesuits. He came to Maryland in 1649, and died in February, 1657, and Ralph Crouch appears to have been his successor. Surgeon Henry Hooper, who died about the year 1650, left a legacy to Ralph Crouch for such "pious uses as he thinks fit."

A complaint was made to the Provincial Court in the spring of 1654, that Luke Gardiner who had been in the service of Father Copley did in "an uncivil, refractory, and insolent manner, detain at his house Eleanor Hatton, sister-in-law of Lt. Richard Banks, and niece of his Lordship's Secretary Thomas Hatton endeavoring as was "probably reported to train her up in the Roman Catholic religion, contrary to the mind and will of her mother and uncle."

Lt. Richard Banks was authorized to go and take her from the custody of Gardiner.

This year Father Francis Fitzherbert, without any companion, sailed for Maryland. The vessel, in which he was a passenger, was exposed to a series of gales. The Jesuit Relation for that year says: "The tempest lasted, in all, two months, whence, the opinion arose, that it was not on account of the violence of the ship, or atmosphere, but was occasioned by the malevolence of witches. Forthwith they seize a little old woman suspected of sorcery, guilty or not guilty, they slay her, suspected of this and after examining her with the strictest scrutiny, very heinous sin." The tragedy is more fully alluded to in the Provincial Records. Mr. Henry Corbyn, a young merchant from London,[1] described the circumstance

[1] Henry Corbyn or Corbin was twenty-five years of age in 1654, and was the founder of the Virginia family of that name. He lived between the Rappahannock and Potomac. In 1657 was the register of the vestry of the Parish. The immigrants Washington came about the same time.

His son Gawin was President of the Council of Virginia and had four daughters, and three sons, one of whom, Richard, in 1754 used his influence to procure young Washington a commission, which he enclosed with the following note:

"Dear George: I inclose you a commission. God prosper you with it. Your friend, Richard Corbin."

to the Governor and Council of Maryland. He was a passenger on the ship Charity, John Bosworth, Master. Two or three weeks before they reached the Chesapeake, it was rumored among the sailors, that Mary Lee, one of the passengers, was a witch, and they asked the Captain to have a trial, but he at first refused. The ship daily became more leaky, and the Captain consulted with Corbyn and Robert Chipsham also a merchant, and to allay the fears of the seamen it was decided to allow an examination.

Two of the seamen, without orders, searched her body and declared she had witch marks. During the night, she was fastened to the capstan, and the next morning, the marks "for the most part were shrunk into her body." The sailors then asked Corbyn to examine her, and she confessed she was a witch. The Captain of the ship retired to his cabin, and the sailors, notwithstanding his protest, took and hung her, and then cast her body in the sea.

Francis Darby, Gent., aged thirty-nine years, deposed, that this statement was correct, and he was probably Father Francis Fitzherbert, as it was common for Jesuits to take another name, when on a journey.[1]

During the sway of the Parliament commissioners, Thomas Mathews, William Boreman, John Pyle, and John Dandy[2] acknowledged their belief in the supremacy of the Pope.

[1] Annapolis manuscript record.

[2] John Dandy had been in Clayborne's employ at Kent Island, and was a violent blacksmith. In October, 1640, he was summoned by the Assembly to answer for misdemeanors. In October, 1657, he was tried

On the 30th of November, 1657, Lord Baltimore agreed to forget past controversies, to omit the clauses in the oath of fidelity, to which the Protestants of the Province objected, and did further promise "that he would never give his assent to the repeal of a law established in Maryland, whereby all persons professing to believe in Jesus Christ have freedom of conscience there," and then the Commissioners of Parliament surrendered their power, and once more he appointed his own officers.

The next year Maryland linked herself with Massachusetts in the persecution of the Quakers.

Toward the latter part of 1657 a ship arrived at Jamestown with Thomas Thurston and Josiah Cole, preachers of the Society of Friends. They were looked upon as disturbers of the peace and imprisoned by the Virginians. After their release they went to Maryland and were kindly received by the Puritans William Durand and William Fuller, and hospitably entertained by Richard Preston of Patuxent[1] and his son-in-law William Berry. As they were conscientiously opposed to swearing, they in the place of judicial oaths, simply affirmed. This fact, and the wearing of their hats, gave offence to Lord Baltimore's officers.

At a court held at Patuxent July 8, 1658, a warrant was issued for Cole and Thurston because they had

for cruelty to a servant causing his death, found guilty and hung on an island at the mouth of Leonard's Creek.

[1] Richard Preston in 1649 came with seven in his family, and entered land for 73 persons.

remained in the Province, above one month, without taking the oath of fidelity. Two weeks later, "taking into consideration the insolent behavior of some people called Quakers, who at the Court, in contempt of an order there made and proclaimed, would presumptuously stand covered," the authorities banished them and they made their way to the Dutch settlement at Manhattan through the Indian country.

Preston and others were fined for entertaining the preachers, and one was whipped for refusing to assist a Sheriff in arresting Thurston.

The council, in 1659, issued an "order to seize and whip them, from constable to constable," until they be sent out of the Province.

Francis Howgill published at London, in 1660, a pamphlet entitled "*The Deceiver of the Nations discovered, and his cruelty made manifest, more especially his cruel works of darkness in Mariland, and Virginia.*"

Alluding to the treatment of Cole and Thurston he remarks:

"The Indians, whom they judged to be heathen, exceeded in kindness, in courtesies, in love, and mercy, unto them, who were strangers, which is a shame to the mad, rash rulers of Mariland that have acted so barbarously to our people, and them that came to visit them in the name of the Lord, that instead of receiving them, rejected them, and made order after order, and warrant after warrant, for pursuing, banishing and whipping of them, who came to them, in the name of the Lord, in such haste, that I have seen fifteen warrants out against one man, in a little time, and in one province."

Josiah Cole, traveling in company with Jacob Lumbrozo, the Jew doctor, in July 1658, asked "whether the Jews did look for a Messiah?" Lumbrozo answered; "Yes." Then Cole asked "Who he was that was crucified at Jerusalem?" The Jew replied: "He was a man." Then the Quaker, asked "How did he do all his miracles?" and the answer was: "He did them by art magic." Cole continued: "How did his disciples do the same miracles, after he was crucified?" The Doctor replied "he taught them his art." Some months after Cole and Thurston were banished, Lumbrozo was arraigned for blasphemy, when he stated to the court, that he "said not any thing scoffingly, or in derogation of him Christians acknowledge for their Messiah," but merely declared his belief as a Jew.

The same year that the Quakers appeared, Father Fitzherbert was arraigned. Henry Coursey, described by Lord Baltimore as "a person of good repute and credit, and well esteemed by all the inhabitants of Maryland, he being of the Church of England," wrote to his Lordship as follows:

"Since I wrote my last to you, I have received a message from Mrs. Gerrard, which is, that Mr. Fitzherbert, hath threatened excommunication to Mr. Gerrard, because he doth not bring to church, his wife and children. And further, Mr. Fitzherbert saith, that he hath written home, to the heads of the Church, in England, and that if it be their judgments to have it so, he will come with a party, and compel them. My Lord, this I offer to your Lordship, as Mrs. Gerrard's relation, who, I think, would not offer to report any such thing, if it were not so. And, my Lord, I thank God, the government of the country is now in your officers' hand, but I think, and have good reasons to think so, that it will not long continue there, if such things be not remedied.

"I told Mr. Fitzherbert of it, about a year since, in private, and also that such things were against the law of the country.

"Yet, his answer was, that he must be directed by his conscience, more than by the law of any country. I do not my Lord, thrust myself upon any business of quarrel, but it is peace and quietness I desire. And I hope, your Lordship hath no other cause but to wish the same, and so I refer the consideration of it to you."

On the 5th of October, 1658, his Lordship's Attorney General, at a Court held at St. Leonard's Creek, presented the following:

"An information of his Lordship's attorney against Francis Fitzherbert, for practising of treason and sedition, and giving out rebellious and mutinous speeches, in this his Lordship's Province of Maryland, and endeavouring, as far as in him lay, to raise distraction and disturbances in this his Lordship's said Province.

"1. Francis Fitzherbert did, on the 24th of August, 1658, traitorously and seditiously, at a general meeting, in arms, of the people of the upper part of Patuxent River, to muster, endeavor to seduce and draw from their religion, the inhabitants there met together."

The second and third charges were of the same purport.

"4. That he hath rebelliously and mutinously said, that if Thomas Gerrard Esq., of the Council, did not come and bring his wife and children to his church, he would come and force them to the Church, contrary to a known Act of Assembly for this Province."

For the prosecution there were several witnesses. A son-in-law of Gerrard, Robert Slye the husband of his daughter Susannah, deposed: That some time in or about July or August in the year 1656, Mr. Fitzherbert being at his house, he asked him, who it was, that raised the report that he had beaten his Irish servants, because they refused to be of the same religion with him. Mr. Fitzherbert replied, that he would not and could not disclose the author, but he further said that Mr. Gerrard had beaten an Irish servant of his, because she refused to be a Protestant, or go to prayer with the family that were so. To which Mr. Slye replied that the story was unfounded.

Mr. Fitzherbert then said, that "Gerrard, although he professed himself a Roman Catholic, yet his life and conversation were not agreeable to his profession, because he brought not his wife and children to the church."

* * * * * * "Mr. Fitzherbert told the deponent further, that if Mr. Gerrard brought not his children freely to his church, nor educated them in the principles of the Romish religion, he would take such a course, that he would undertake their education in Mr. Gerrard's own house, whether Mr. Gerrard would give way thereunto or no."

To the charges Fitzherbert demurred.

"1. Neither denying or confessing the matter here objected, since by the very first law of this country, Holy Church, within this province, shall have, and enjoy all her rights, liberties and franchises, wholly and without blemish, amongst which that of preaching and teaching is not the least.

"Neither imports it what church is there meant; since by the true intent of the Act concerning Religion, every church professing to believe in God the Father, Son, and Holy Ghost, is accounted Holy Church here.

2. Because, by the act entitled, An Act concerning Religion, it is provided that no person whatsoever, professing to believe in Jesus Christ, shall be molested, for or in respect of his or her religion, or the free exercise thereof. And undoubtedly preaching and teaching, is the free exercise of every Churchman's religion. And upon this I crave judgment."

The Court decided that the charges of mutiny and sedition had not been proved. Gerrard, it was evident, was not a Roman Catholic at heart.

After the compromise by Lord Baltimore with the

Parliament Commissioners, he appointed Josias Fendall, Governor. On the 28th of February 1659, the Assembly convened at Thomas Gerrard's house, and on the first of March, the lower branch of the legislature adjourned to the residence of Robert Slye, his son in-law, and declared itself the highest court of jurisdiction in the Province. Gerrard and his fellow councillor Utie, with the Governor, assented to this position, and the upper house ceased to sit as a distinct body, and the Assembly as the source of power issued commissions.

Soon after this republican movement, Gerrard seems to have changed his residence to Virginia.[1]

The Provincial Records contain an account of the hanging of a witch, in 1659, in the presence of John Washington the first American ancestor of George Washington, as he was coming from England. Wash-

[1] He lived at Masthotick Creek, the southern boundary of Westmoreland Co., Va. On March 3d 1670 he entered into a compact with his neighbors John Lee, Henry Corbin and Isaac Allerton, to build a banqueting house at or near their respective lands.

John Lee was a relative of Col. Richard Lee a friend of Parliament during the civil war. Isaac Allerton graduated in 1650 at Harvard. His mother, Fear Brewster, was the wife of Isaac Allerton Sr. who came with her father, the leader of the Puritans, to Plymouth Rock in the May Flower. Hancock, the son of Richard Lee, married the daughter of Isaac Allerton, thus, on the banks of the Potomac, at an early day, the families of those who were useful and faithful to the interests of the commonwealth of England intermarried.

In the will of Thomas Gerrard dated Feb. 5, 1672, he expressed a wish to be buried in Maryland, by the side of his first wife Susanna Snow, and appointed Major Isaac Allerton, John Lee, and John Cooper to settle his estate.

On Herrman's Map of Virginia and Maryland, engraved by Faithorne, drawn in 1670, Allerton's plantation is marked.

ington complained to the authorities of Maryland against Edward Prescott for hanging a witch, and the proceedings of the Court were as follows:

"Present October 5, 1659, at Mr. George Reade's house Josias Fendall Esq., Governor Philip Calvert Esq. Secretary, Capt. William Stone, Mr. Thomas Gerrard, Col. Nathaniel Utye, Mr. Baker Brooke, and Mr. Edward Lloyd.

"Whereas John Washington[1] of Westmoreland County hath made comp^{lt} ag'st Edward Prescott, Merch't Accusing ye s'd Prescott of ffelony unto ye Gouvernor of this Province, alleging how that hee ye

[1] J. L. Chester, Esq., of London, a careful investigator, has pointed out the mistake of Sparks, Irving and others in supposing that John Washington was the son of Lawrence of Sulgrave.

General Washington in a letter to the Earl of Buchan states that his ancestors were related to the Fairfaxes.

Henry Fairfax, Sheriff of Yorkshire, and Richard Washington married sisters, Anna and Eleanora Harrison of South Cave, Yorkshire.

William, son of Henry Fairfax, became President of the Council of Virginia, and his daughter married Lawrence, the brother of General George Washington. Henry Washington had a son Richard, who was in Lincoln's Inn. (See *Fairfaxes of America,* Munsell, Albany, 1868, p. 58.)

Mr. Chester in a letter to me, writes of this Richard, as follows: "In reply to your inquiries about Henry Washington of South Cave, I am able to say that he did have a son Richard. Henry Washington was married to Eleanor Harrison in 1689 and this Richard was their eldest son, born the next year. His father died in 1718, and the widow lived in St. Andrews' Holborn, London. She had seven children, two were baptized at South Cave, and five at Doncaster or in London."

It is probable that John Washington was one of the sons of Richard of Lincoln's Inn, and grandson of Henry, and that the Richard Washington of London, with whom General George Washington frequently corresponded, was his cousin, and the son of another child of Richard of Lincoln's Inn.

s'd Prescott hanged a witch, on his ship, as hee was outward bound from England within the last yeare, upon wich complaynt of ye s'd Washington the Gov'r caused ye s'd Edward Prescott to bee arrested. Taking bond for his appearance att this Provincial Court of 40,000 lbs. Tobacco. Gyving moreover notice to ye s'd Washington, by letter of his proceedings therein, a copie of wich l'tre, with the said Washington's answere thereto are as followeth:

"Mr. Washington, Upon yo'r complaynt to mee y't Mr. Prescott did in his voyage from England hither cause a woman to bee executed for a witch, I have caused him be apprehended uppon suspition of ffelony and I've intend to bind him over to ye Provincial Court to answer it, where I doe allso expect you to bee to make good ye charge. Hee will be called uppon his Tryal ye 4th or 5th of October next, at ye Court, to be held there at Patux't neare Mr Fenwick's house, where I suppose you will not fayle to bee. Witnesses examined in Virginia will bee of no value here in this case, for they must be face to face, with ye party accused, or they stand for nothing. I thought good to acquaynt you with this, that you may not come unprovided.

"This at present S^r^ is all from

Yo'r ffriend

JOSIAS FENDALL.

29th September.

"Hon'ble S'r. Yo^rs of this 29th instant, this day I received. I am sorry y't my extraordinary occasions, will not permit me to bee at ye next Provincial Court to bee held at Mary Land ye 4th of this next month.

Because then, God willing, I intend to gett my young sonne baptized.[1] All ye company and Gossips[2] being already invited. Besides in this short time witnesses cannot bee gott to come over. But if Mr. Prescott bee bound to answer at ye next Provinciall Court after this, I shall doe what lyeth in my power, to get them over. Sr I shall desire you for to acquaynt mee, whether Mr. Prescott be bound over to ye next Court, and when ye Court is, that I may have sometime for to provide evidence.

Yo'r ffriend & Serv't,

30 Sept. 1659. JOHN WASHINGTON.

"To which complaint Edward Prescott submitting himself to trial, denied not, that one Elizabeth Richardson was hanged on his ship, as he was outward

---

[1] The Rev. Mr. Cole was the first clergyman on the Virginia side of the Potomac and at this time lived at Matschotick, Westmoreland, a near neighbor of the pioneer settlers Lee, Gerrard, Washington, and Isaac Allerton the grandson of William Brewster, the head of the Puritans of Plymouth Rock.

[2] Gossips, sponsors for an infant in baptism from the Anglo-Saxon *God* and *syb* or *sip* kindred or affinity. Verstegan says, "Our Christian ancestors understanding a spiritual affinity to grow between the parents, and such as undertook for the child at baptism, called each other by the name of *God-sib*, which is as much to say, as that they were *sib* together, that is of kin together through God."

bound, the last year, from England, and near the West Isles by Master John Greene, and the company, hung."

No one appearing to deny this plea, that he was not responsible for the acts of Greene and his crew, the accused was discharged.

THE CONDITION OF RELIGION FROM THE ACCESSION OF CHARLES THE SECOND UNTIL A.D. 1700.

THE absence of towns, and the separation of plantations by numerous streams and dense forests were unfavorable to the upbuilding of churches. As there were no centres of population, the accession of Charles the Second found only one clergyman, who was more than sixty years of age, employed in the duties of his profession.

The Society of Friends with their migratory evangelists of both sexes, discovered a field in Maryland, ripe for their labors. The non-conformists who came from Virginia, as they were not able in their scattered residences, to support a pastor, willingly listened to preaching of the Gospel, by the new sect developed by the agitations of the Cromwellian era. Among the earliest, to brave the discomforts of traveling in the wilderness, to speak of the love of Jesus, for sinful humanity, was Elizabeth Harris, the wife of a prosperous London merchant. After her return to England, a convert named Robert Clarkson wrote as follows:

"Dear Heart: I salute thee in the tender love of the Father, which moved thee, towards us, and do own thee, to have been a minister by the good will of God, to bear outward testimony to the inward truth on me and others, even as many as the Lord in tender love and mercy, did give an ear to hear. Praise be to his name forever, of which and of life, God hath made my wife partaker with me, and hath established our hearts in his fear. And likewise, Ann Dorsey, in a more large measure; her husband I hope abideth faithful; likewise John Baldwin and Henry Carline. Charles Balye, the young man who was with us, at our parting, abides convinced, and several others, in these parts, where he dwells. Elizabeth Beaseley abides as she was, when thou wast here. Thomas Cole and William Cole[1] have made open confession of the truth, likewise Henry Woolchurch, and many others, suffer the reproachful name. William Fuller abides unmoved.[2] I know not but that William Durand doth the like, he frequents our meeting but seldom. * * * * * We have disposed of the most part of the books which were

[1] William Cole became a Quaker preacher and in 1662 was imprisoned at Jamestown for violating the statutes. *Besse*, vol. 2, p. 138.

[2] William Fuller was appointed on July 22, 1654, by the Agents of Parliament, with Richard Preston, William Durand, and others, Commissioners for the government of Maryland. When Stone and his forces appeared on Sunday, March 25, 1655, Fuller at the head of one hundred and twenty men marched around the peninsula in the southern suburb of Annapolis, with the colors of the Commonwealth of England flying. A skirmish took place and the color-bearer was killed. This led to a short and sharp engagement in which the Baltimore party under Stone was completely routed, threw down their arms, and begged for mercy.

In adopting the tenets of the Society of Friends, Fuller relinquished military exercises.

sent, so that all parts are furnished and every one that desires it, may have benefit by them, at Herring Creek, Roade River, South River, all about Severn the Broad Neck and thereabout, the Seven Mountains, and Kent. With my dear love, I salute thy husband, and rest with thee and the gathered ones, in the eternal word, which abideth for ever."

Thus in 1657, before the arrival of Cole and Thurston, to which allusion has been made, the planting of Quakerism had commenced, and Preston, Berry and the more sober-minded citizens, listened gladly to the tenets of the society.

In the autumn of 1663, Alice Ambrose[1] and Mary Tomkins, were at the Cliffs of the Chesapeake, in Calvert County, having retreated from New England, where, says Bishop, they "suffered thirty-two stripes apiece, with a nine corded whip, three knots in each cord, being drawn up to the pillory, in such an uncivil manner, as is not to be rehearsed, with a rnnning knot about their hands, the very first lash of which, drew the blood, and made it run down, in abundance, from their breasts."

From thence, they wrote to George Fox, in England, telling him of their "good service and sufferings for the Lord."

John Burnyeat of Cumberland, in 1665, was impelled to leave England, and visit Maryland, where he

[1] Alice Ambrose afterwards married John Gary, supposed to have been the son of the wife of Dr. Peter Sharpe, who was a widow Gary.

held large meetings and "Friends were greatly comforted, and several were convinced." In 1671, he made a second visit, accompanied by Daniel Gould of Rhode Island. One day in 1672, as he was about to sail for England, unexpectedly to all, a ship from Jamaica appeared in the Patuxent river, having on board George Fox, whose name is so prominently identified with the religious history of the seventeenth century, and several other Quakers, one of whom was William Edmundson, a native of Westmoreland, and once a soldier in Cromwell's army.

Feeling that his stay must be brief, the feet of Fox had scarcely touched the sands of the Patuxent before he began to preach. For four days he expounded his doctrines, with singular clearness, and with a voice remarkable for mellowness, prayed from the depths of his soul, and as a result, five or six justices of the peace, and many "world's people," who came from curiosity, went away from the meetings, much interested.

Partly by land, and partly by water, he hastened to the Cliffs, in Calvert County, and addressed a large assembly, and then, crossing the Chesapeake Bay, crowds gathered to listen, and a judge's wife was frank to say "she had rather hear him once, than the priests a thousand times."

Returning to the western shore, he spoke at the Severn, where the numbers were so great that no building was large enough to hold the congregation.

The next day he was at Abraham Birkhead's, six or seven miles distant, and there the Speaker of the Assembly was convinced; then mounting his horse he rode to Dr. Peter Sharpe's at the Cliffs of Calvert. Here was a "heavenly meeting," many of the upper sort of people present, and a wife of one of the Governor's councillors was convinced.

Some Roman Catholics came to deride but they had no heart to oppose. From thence he rode eighteen miles to James Preston's, on the Patuxent, where an Indian chief and some of his tribe came to see the strange man who was lifting up his voice, like John the Baptist, in the wilderness. After a tour to Virginia and Carolina he came back to Preston's on the twenty-seventh of the eleventh month, 1672, and soon began to travel amid snow storms, to declare the truth in Christ, as he understood it. Taking a boat at the Cliffs, for the Eastern Shore, he was obliged to pass a night without fire. In Somerset County, he held a meeting at Anamessex, and then proceeded to Hunger's Creek, Little Choptank, Tredhaven, Wye, and to John Taylor's on Kent Island.

His labors had been incessant; neither wintry sleet nor the burning sun detained. He forded streams, slept in the woods, and in barns, with as much serenity, as in the comfortable houses of his friends, and was truly a wonder unto many.

Before he returned to England, he rested a few days at the Cliffs, went up to Annapolis, attended the meeting of the Provincial Assembly, and early in 1673, sailed for his native land.[1]

Edmundson proceeded to North Carolina, while Fox visited New England. In 1672 the former, upon his return, visited the valley of the James River, called upon Governor Berkeley and met with Major General Richard Bennett, late Commissioner of Parliament for Maryland. He writes in his Journal:

"As I returned, it was laid upon me to visit the Governor Sir William Barclay, and to speak with him about Friend's sufferings. I went about six miles out of my way, to speak with him, accompanied by William Garrett, an honest, ancient Friend. I told the Governor, that I came from Ireland, where his brother was Lord Lieutenant, who was kind to our Friends; and if he had any service for me to his brother, I would willingly do it; and as his brother was kind to our Friends in Ireland I hoped he would be so to our Friends in Virginia.

"He was very peevish, and brittle, and I could fasten nothing on him, with all the soft arguments I could use. * * * * * *

"The next day, was the men's meeting at William Wright's house, the justice [Taverner] went to the meeting, about eight or nine miles, and several other

[1] After Fox arrived in England he sent a copy of the Writings of Edward Burroughs to several gentlemen, among others to Judge Stevens and Justices Johnson and Coleman of Anamessex, Maryland, and to Major General Bennett, Lt. Col. Waters, and Col. Thomas Dew of Nansemond Co., Virginia. *Bowden*, vol. 1, p. 381.

persons came to the meeting, particularly Richard Bennett, alias Major General Bennett. Justice Tavern-er's wife came to me and told me that the Major General and others were below staying to speak with me; so I went down to them. They were courteous, and said, they only stayed to see me, and acknowledge what I had spoken in the meeting, was truth. I told them, the reason of our Friends drawing apart from them, was to lay down a method, to provide for our poor widows, and fatherless children. * * * * * * * * * The Major General replied, he was glad to hear, there was such care and order among us. He further said, he was a man of great estate, and many of our Friends poor men; therefore, he desired to contribute with them. He likewise asked me, how I was treated by the Governor? I told him, that he was brittle and peevish, and I could get nothing fastened on him. He asked me 'If the Governor called me dog, rogue,' etc? I said, 'No.' 'Then' said he 'you took him in his best humor, those being his usual terms, when he is angry, for he is an enemy to every appearance of good.'

"They were tender and loving, and we parted so, the Major General desiring to see me at his house, which I was willing to do, and accordingly went.

"He was a solid, wise man, receiving the truth, and died in the same, leaving two Friends executors."

Dr. Peter Sharpe of the Cliffs, whose name is perpetuated by Sharpe's Island, in the Chesapeake, in his will, made in 1672, says: "I give to Friends, in ye ministry, viz: Alice Gary, William Cole, and Sarah Mash, if then in being; Winlock Christeson and his wife, John Burnyeat, and Daniel Gould, in money or goods, at the choice of my executors, forty shillings worth apiece; also for a perpetual standing, a horse for the use of Friends in ye Ministry, and to be placed at a convenient place for their use."

The Wenlock Christeson of the will, or Christopherson, is the same person, who when sentenced to death at Boston, uttered the memorable words: "For the last man that was put to death here, are five come in his room. If you have power, take my life from me, God can raise up the same principle in ten of his servants, and send them among you, in my room."

In 1674, Christeson, with others, ask the Provincial Assembly for permission to affirm, instead of taking the usual oaths prescribed by law.

The Rev. John Yeo of the Church of England appears in Maryland in 1675, and was disturbed by the movements of the Quakers, Mennonite Baptists, Roman Catholics and other non-conformists. From the Patuxent, on the 25th of May, 1676, he wrote the following letter of lamentations to Sheldon, Archbishop of Canterbury.

"Most Reverend Father: Be pleased to pardon this presumption of mine, in presenting to y^{or} serious notice these rude and undigested lines, w^{ch} (with humble submission) are to acquaint y^{or} Grace, with ye deplorable estate and condition of the Province of Maryland, for want of an established ministry.

"Here are in this Province ten or twelve thousand souls, and but three Protestant ministers of us, y^t are conformable to ye doctrine and discipline of ye Church of England.

"Others there are (I must confess) y^t runne before they are sent, and pretend they are ministers of the Gospell, y^t never had a legall call or ordination to such an holy office; neither indeed are they qualified for it, being, for the most part, such as never understood anything of learning, and yet take upon them to be dispensers of the Word, and to administer ye Sacrament of Baptism; and sow seeds of division amongst ye people, and no law provided for ye suppression of such in this Province.

"Society here is in great necessitie of able and learned men to comfort the gainsayers, especially having soe many profest enemies as the Popish Priests and Jesuits are who are incouraged and provided for. And ye Quaker takes care and provides for those y^t are speakers in their conventicles; but noe care is taken, or provision made, for the building up Christians in the Protestant Religion; by means whereof, not only many dayly fall away, either to Popery, Quakerism, or Fanaticisme, but also the Lord's Day is prophaned, religion despised, and all notorious vices committed; so that it is become a Sodom of uncleanness, and a pest house of iniquity.

"I doubt not, but y^{or} Grace will take it into consideration, and do y^{or} utmost for our eternall welfare; and now is y time y^{t} y^{or} Grace may be an instrument of universall reformation, with greatest facility. Cecilius, Lord Barron Baltemore, and absolute Proprietor of Maryland being dead, and Charles Lord Barron Baltemore and our Governor being bound for England this year, as I am informed, to receive a further confirmation of y Province from His Majestie, at wch time, I doubt not, but y^{or} Grace may soe prevaile with, as y^{t} a maintenance for a Protestant ministry may be established as well in this Province, as in Virginia, Barbados, and all other His Majesties plantations in West Indies; and then there will be encouragement for able men to come amongst us, and y^{t} some person may have power to examine all such ministers as shall be admitted into any county or parish, in w^{t} Diocis, and by w^{t} Bishop they were ordained, and to exhibit their l'rs of Orders to testifie the same, as y^{t} I think the generalitie of the people may be brought by degrees to a uniformitie; provided we had more ministers y^{t} were truly conformable to our mother ye Church, and none but such suffered to preach amongst us. As for my own p^{t}, God is my witness, I have done my utmost indeavor in order thereunto, and shall (by God's assistance) whiles I have a being here, give manifest proof of my faithful obedience to the Canons and Constitution of our sacred mother.

"Yet one thing cannot be obtained here, viz, Consecration of Churches and Church-yards, to ye end y^{t} Christians might be decently buried together, whereas now, they bury in the severall plantations where they lived: unless y^{or} Grace thought it sufficient to give a Dispensation to some pious ministers together with ye manner and forme, to doe the same. And confident I am y^{t} you will not be wanting in any thing y^{t} may tend most to God's glorie, and the good of the Church, by wch you will engage thousands of soules to pray for y^{or} Grace's everlasting happiness."

The Archbishop of Canterbury referred Yeo's letter to Compton, Bishop of London, who on the 17th of July, 1677, wrote: "In Maryland, there is no settled maintenance for the ministry at all, the want whereof does occasion a total want of ministers and divine worship, except among those of the Romish belief, who 'tis conjectured do not amount to one of a hundred of the people."

Lord Baltimore to the application of the Bishop replied, that the Act of 1649, confirmed in 1676, tolerated and protected every sect, and continued "Four ministers of the Church of England are in possession of plantations which offered them a decent subsistence.[1] That, from the various religious tenets of the

[1] The Rev. Wm. Wilkinson died in 1663, and Francis Doughty was probably dead. The four ministers referred to were perhaps Yeo; Coode a political agitator; the minister sent out by Charles the Second referred to in letter of Mary Taney, see page 160; and Matthew Hill. The last was a native of Yorkshire, educated at Magdalene College and Rector at Thirsk, but ejected by the Act of Uniformity. He came about 1669 to Charles County, Maryland. His father-in-law Walter Bayne had entered a tract of 5000 acres called Barbadoes, on the east side of the main fresh run of Port Tobacco creek. Calamy says, after he was settled and had bright hopes "new troubles arose. He was a good scholar, a lively preacher, and of a free and generous spirit."

members of the Assembly, it would be extremely difficult, if not impossible, to induce it to consent to a law, that shall oblige any sect to maintain other ministers, than its own."

Yeo does not appear to have been remarkable for learning, or Christian charity.[1] In December, 1677,

---

[1] The following letter is preserved among the New York MS. Records at Albany, addressed "To Mr. Henry Smith at Capt. Greges his house, present These at N. Yorke."

Whorekill, November the 14th, 1678.

Worthy Sir,

Yours of the 5th I Rec'd the 7th Instant in w[ch] you desired me to minde Capt. Avery, to swear the Evidences, that these depositions might be sent to you ; in order to your desire, I did the same day write a warrant, and Carried it myselfe to Avery, and he signed it and Imediately I ride wth it to the Sherieffe who wth all expedition served it upon most of the evidences, but the day before they were to appeare to give in there Testimony, the s'd Avery came to your house. and did abuse me at a very high Rate & Thretning to send me to Yorke to answer w[t] I had done, viz., written a warrant w[ch] did, as he said, properly belong to the clerke's office for bringing it to him to signe when he was as he pretended Drunke (to his Creditt be it spoken) at w[ch] time, he absolutely refused to examine any evidence, unless it were by express order of the Governor, notwithstanding the warrant was for them, to give in there Evidence, in the behalfe of our Sovraigne Lord, the king and Avery did then take away the warrant and Toare his name out it, neither would he Returne it any more to the sherife, but I wth much Intreaty and some thretning gott a Coppy of it Attested, a Coppy of w[ch] I have sent you.

Avery is very greate with Helms & there gange: there is never a Barrell the better Herring amongst severall of them, they are very Briske againe now, since the sloop brought noe order for there coming to Yorke ; and now Helms saith, that all y[e] men in the Countrey shall never gett him to Yorke. Avery sideing with them, you are daily abused, and I am counted amongst them, the worst of men. Helms cannot leave his Tricks yet, for when M[r] Clark's Goods came down, out of ½ doz. Reapehooks he Borrowed six, for he left not one ; he kept them severall dayes, till at last old Tom told Clarke's serv'ts that his M[r] had them, and went and fetched y[e] hooks to them.

he moved from the Patuxent to Whorekill, what is now called Lewes, in Delaware, and there became involved in local disputes. The following certificate dated March 28, 1678, was given by the Court, on the Delaware.

"John Yeo, minister, being lately arrived out of Maryland, appeared in Court, and exhibited and produced his letters of ordination and license to read divine service, administer the holy sacraments, and preach the word of God according to the laws and constitution of the Church of England.

"The Court accepts said John Yeo, upon the approbation of his honor the Governor, to be maintained by the free willing gifts, whereunto, the said John Yeo declared himself contented."

In 1680 he was arraigned for mutinous expressions against the Duke of York, the town and the Court, but was acquitted. After this he appears to have returned to Calvert County, Maryland, and from thence,

---

He hath also lately bought hoggs * * * * * * * * * he did one the 14th of the last month declare before some people y[t] y[e] king did allow dutch waights and measures to pass in this countrey, but the Governor did cheate the countrey of it, w[ch] of y[e] Scurrolous speeches y[e] 26th of 8[bris]. The day after our arrivall at y[e] Whorekill sold Corn[s] the Clark's place for one quart of wine, at M[r] Vines his house & one the Tuesday after he acted as clarke at y[e] Court. I heartily long to see you home and then I doubt not but all will be well. M[rs] Smith presents her Affections to you, she is mightily troubled at your absence. I have seen very few women Grieve more for the death of A husband, than she grieves for your Long absence, Espetially in that you came not with the sloops. Thus not doubting, but that you will in a short time ——— all your Enimies and Returne victorious, I am, Sir, Your Ready friend and Serv't, JOHN YEO."

in 1682, went to Baltimore County where, about the year 1686, he died.

Another form of Christian faith was planted in Maryland, in 1680, and the Province became the rival of Holland, in varieties of religious belief, and to it were applicable the lines of Andrew Marvell, written concerning Amsterdam.

"Sure, when Religion, did itself embark
And from the East, would Westward steer its bark,
It struck; and splitting on this unknown ground,
Each one thence pillaged the first piece he found;
Hence, Amsterdam, Turk, Christian, Pagan, Jew,
Staple of sects, and mint of schism grew;
That bank of conscience, where not one, so strange
Opinion. but finds credit and exchange,
In vain for Catholics, ourselves we bear,
The Universal Church is only there."

The visionary but pure-minded priest Labadie, after he withdrew from the Church of Rome, urged some peculiar views, which were not acceptable to the Reformed Churches, and after much persecution, he and his adherents were sheltered in Friesland, a province of the Netherlands.

In 1679 Danker and Sluyter were sent by the Labadists to select a site for a colony in North America. Arriving at Manhattan, now New York City, on October the twentieth, they became acquainted with Ephraim Herrman, clerk of the Court of Newcastle and Upland on the Delaware River, and son of Augustine Herrman, the proprietor of Bohemia Manor, in Maryland.

With him, these delegates descended the Delaware, passed Tacony, a Swedish settlement, now a suburb of Philadelphia, and rested on Tinicum Island, a few miles below that city.

While the Labadists were neat in dress, frugal in living, and like the Quakers depended much upon the inspiration of the Holy Spirit, yet there was no affinity between these religionists. Danker, in his journal, says, that while he was at a Swede's house, on the Island, "there arrived three Quakers, of whom one was the great prophetess, who travels through the whole country, in order to quake. She lives in Maryland, and forsakes husband and children, plantation, and all, and goes off for this purpose. She had been to Boston,[1] and was there arrested by the authorities, in account of her quaking."

On the 1st of December, the Labadists arrived at the plantation of Caspar, another son of Herrman, situated between the Delaware River and Chesapeake Bay. From thence they went to Augustine Herrman's, "the uppermost plantation of Maryland, that is as high up as it is yet inhabited by Christians."[2]

Danker, on Sunday, the 30th of December, 1679, writes in his journal:

"Augustine is a Bohemian and formerly lived in the Manathans, and had possession of farms and planta-

[1] Perhaps Alice Gary, see page 143.

[2] Augustine Herrman a native of Prague came to Manhattan about 1649 as clerk or factor to the brothers Gabri. In 1650 he was one of the selectmen of Manhattan.

tions, but for some reason, I know not what, disagreeing with the Dutch Governor Stuyvesant, he repaired to this place, which is laid down upon a complete map which he has made of Maryland and Virginia, where he is very well acquainted, which map he has dedicated to the King.[1]

"In consequence of his having done the people a great service, he has been presented with a tract of land of ten hundred or twelve hundred acres, which he knowing where the best land is, has chosen up here, and given it the name Bohemia."

He adds: "He was very miserable both in body and soul. His plantation was going much into decay, as well as his body, for want of attention. There was not a Christian man to serve him, as the term is, but only negroes."[2]

On another page, speaking of the children, he writes: "They are all of a Dutch mother, after whose death, the father married an English woman, the most willful and despicable creature that can be found. He

---

[1] The Map alluded to is called "Virginia and Maryland as it is planted aud inhabited this present year 1670; surveyed and exactly drawne by the only labours and endeavours of Augustine Herrman, Bohemiensis."

It was the only map engraved by Faithorne who was distinguished for crayon portraits, and delicate copper plate engraving. The only one I have ever seen, is in the British Museum. It is in four folio sheets, and at the bottom, has a portrait of Herrman. Lately the state of Virginia has had a reduced copy, printed by the litho-photographic process.

[2] Negroes were considered infidels, and not allowed to be baptized, as baptism was supposed to give freedom to slaves. The Assembly of 1715 enacted the following:

is a very godless person, and the wife by her wickedness has compelled all the children to leave the father's house and live elsewhere."

Several of the children embraced the tenets of Labadie.[1] After Danker returned to Manhattan, he wrote that Ephraim Herrman was on a visit, and with his wife rejoicing in their faith. Under date of the 4th of June he writes: "Visited by Ephraim and one Peter Beyaert, a deacon of the Dutch Church, a very good soul, whom the Lord had begun to trouble and enlighten."

Danker and Sluyter returned to Friesland and a colony was organized to proceed to Maryland. The

---

"Forasmuch as many people have neglected to baptize their negroes, or to suffer them to be baptized, on a vague apprehension, that negroes by receiving sacrament of baptism are manumitted or set free.

"Be it, hereby, further declared, and enacted, that no negro or negroes, by receiving the holy sacrament of baptism, is thereby manumitted or set free, nor hath any right or title to manumission, more than he or they had before, any law, usage, or custom to the contrary notwithstanding."

[1] He was married on Dec. 10, 1650, to a Dutch woman at Manhattan, and she had the following children

Ephraim George	baptized	Sept. 1, 1652.
Caspar	"	July 2, 1656.
Anna Magaritta	"	March 2, 1658.
Judith	"	May 7, 1660.
Francina	"	March 12, 1662.

By an Act of the Maryland Assembly in 1666, these were all naturalized.

Anna Margaritta married Matthias Vanderhuyden, and her daughter Anna Francina, became the second wife of Edward Shippen a wealthy Quaker of Philadelphia, who in 1675, had been whipped on Boston Common, for speaking against the established religion. A descendant of this Edward Shippen was the wife of Benedict Arnold, the traitor to the American cause during the war of the Revolution.

company arrived in New York on the 27th of July, 1683. Deacon Peter Bayard the hatter and nephew of Governor Stuyvesant, leaving his family, united with them.

On the 11th of August, 1684, Augustus Herrman makes a deed, conveying certain lands to Peter Sluyter, Joseph Dankaerts, Petrus Bayard of New York, John Moll and Arnold de la Grange of Delaware.

The Labadist colony, like all communist organizations, had a brief existence. Bownas, as a Quaker preacher, describes a visit to it, in 1702:

"When supper came in, it was placed upon a long table, in a large room, where, when all things were ready, about twenty men or upwards came in, at a call, but no women.

"We all sat down, they placing me and my companion near the head of the table, and having paused a short space, one pulled off his hat, but not the rest till a short space after; and then one after another they all pulled their hats off, and as that occurred sat silent, uttered no words that we could hear, for half or quarter of an hour; and as they did not uncover at once, so did not they cover again, at once, but, as they put on their hats, fell to eating, not regarding those who were still uncovered, so that it might be two minutes' time, or more, between the first and last putting off their hats.

"I, afterward, queried with my companion concerning the reason of their conduct, and he gave, for this answer, that they held it unlawful to pray, till they felt some inward motive for the purpose, and that secret prayer was more acceptable than to utter words.

"I, likewise, queried, 'If they had no women among them?' He told me they had, but the women all by themselves; having all things in common, respecting their household affairs, so that none could claim any more right than another to any part of the stock. All men, whether rich or poor, must put what they had in the common stock, and likewise, if they had a mind to leave, they must go out empty handed.'

"They frequently expound the Scriptures among themselves; and being a very large family, in all upward of one hundred men, women, and children, they carried on the manufacturing of linen, and had a very large plantation of corn, tobacco, flax and hemp, together with cattle of several kinds."

In 1681, a sum of money was paid out of the secret service fund of the king for the payment of the passage of the Rev. Jonathan Sanders, to Maryland;[1] and in 1683 the Rev. Duel Pead[2] and William Mullett were designated for labor in the Province.

---

[1] There is among the British Public Records a recommendation of the Rev. Ambrose Sanderson by the Privy Council dated Oct. 8th, 1681, as a suitable minister for Protestant subjects, addressed to the Proprietary of Maryland, but there is no evidence that he came to America nor do we find any mention of Jonathan Saunders.

[2] In Westminster Abbey on April 18, 1663, Paul Thorndyke, son of John Thorndyke of New England, aged twenty, ancestor of the American family; and, Duell Pead, one of the King's scholars about sixteen years of age, was baptized by the Dean, publicly, in the font, then

In 1685, according to a letter of Mary Taney, wife of the sheriff of Calvert County, the ancestor of the late distinguished Chief Justice of the United States of America, there was no Church of England minister then residing in her vicinity. Under date of the 14th of July she wrote to the Archbishop of Canterbury.

"May it please your Grace; I am now to repeat my request to your Grace, for a church in the place of Maryland where I live; but first I humbly thank your Grace, that you were pleased to hear so favorably, and own my desires very reasonable, and to encourage the inhabitants to make a petition to the King.

Our want of a minister, and the many blessings our Saviour designed us by them, is a misery, which I and a numerous family, and many others in Maryland, have groaned under. We are seized with extreme horror when we think, that for want of the Gospel our children and posterity are in danger to be condemned to infidelity or to apostacy. We do not question God's care of us, but think your Grace, and the Right Reverend, your Bishops, the proper instruments

---

newly set up." In 1664 he was a member of Trinity College, Cambridge, and in 1671 was Chaplain on board H. M. ship Rupert, Among the entries in the Camden Society's volume entitled "Secret Services of Chas. II and James II" under date of 14 June, 1683, is the payment of £20 to Duell Pead, Clerk, bounty to him for the charge of his transportation to Maryland." If he ever came to America, he did not long remain, for in 1691 he was licensed as Curate or Minister of St. James, Clerkenwell. See *Chester's Westminster Abbey Registers.* He had a son Deuel, who in 1712, received the degree of A.M. from Cambridge University, and was probably the clergyman who was settled at Annapolis, Maryland, and also preached in Virginia.

of so great a blessing to us. We are not, I hope, so foreign to your jurisdiction, but we may be owned your stray flock; however, the commission to go, and baptize, and teach all nations, is large enough. But I am sure we are, by a late custom upon tobacco, sufficiently acknowledged subjects of the King of England, and therefore by his protection, not only our persons and estates, but of what is more dear to us, our religion. I question not but that your Grace is sensible, that without a temple it will be impracticable, neither can we expect a minister to hold out, to ride ten miles in a morning, and before he can dine, ten more, and from house to house, in hot weather, will dishearten a minister, if not kill him.

Your Grace is so sensible of our sad condition, and for your place and piety's sake, have so great an influence on our most religious and gracious King, that if I had not your Grace's promise to depend upon, I could not question your Grace's intercession and prevailing. £500 or £600 for a church, with some small encouragement for a minister, will be extremely less charge, than honor, to his Majesty.

One church settled according to the Church of England, which is the sum of our request, will prove a nursery of religion and loyalty through the whole Province. But your Grace needs no arguments from me, but only this, it is in your power to give us many happy opportunities to praise God for this and innumerable mercies, and to importune His goodness, to bless his

Majesty, with a long and prosperous reign over us, and long continue to your Grace, the great blessing of being an instrument of good to his Church. And now that I may be no more troublesome, I humbly entreat your pardon to the well meant zeal of

Your Grace's most obedient servant,

MARY TANEY.

Accompanying this letter was the following Petition :

"To the Most Reverend the Archbishops, and the rest of the Right Reverend the Bishops, the humble petition of Mary Taney, on the behalf of herself and others his Majesty's subjects inhabitants of the Province of Maryland.

"*Sheweth*, That your petitioner in her petition to the King's Majesty, setting forth That the said Province, being without a church or any settled ministry, to the great grief of all his Majesty's loyal subjects there, his late Majesty, King Charles the Second of blessed memory, was graciously pleased to send over thither, a minister, and a parcel of Bibles, and other church books of considerable value, in order to the settlement of a church and ministry there.

"That the said minister dying, and the inhabitants who have no other trade but in tobacco, being so very poor that they are not able to maintain a minister, chiefly by reason of his Majesty's customs, here upon tobacco, which causes the inhabitants to sell it there, to the merchants, at their own rates. By means whereof so good a work as was intended by his said late Majesty is like to miscarry, to the utter ruin of many poor souls, unless supplied by his Majesty.

"Praying his Majesty, that a certain parcel of tobacco, of one hundred hogsheads or thereabouts, of the growth or product of the said Province, may be custom free, for and towards the maintenance of an orthodox divine, at Colvert Town, in the said Province, or otherwise allow maintenance for a minister there.

"Your petitioner, therefore, most humbly prays, that your Lordships will be pleased, not only to mediate with his Majesty and in your petitioner's behalf request him to grant her desire in such petition, but likewise, that your Lordships will vouchsafe to contribute towards the building of a church at Colvert Town, as your Lordships in charity and goodness shall think meet."

A little while after this petition was received, on the 29th of September, 1685, a sum of money was given from the secret service fund of the King, to defray the passage of the Rev. Paul Bertrand to Maryland.

There is preserved the report of this clergyman dated the 12th of September, 1689, written in French, addressed to the Bishop of London, which describes the condition of religion in the province at that time.[1]

Year after year the members of the Society of Friends increased, and were respected. In a reply to

[1] See Stevens's Catalogue of Manuscripts presented by George Peabody to Maryland Historical Society.

a petition, that Quakers might be allowed to affirm, in the place of taking the usual oath, the Upper House of the Assembly on the 6th of September, 1681, took the following action:

"Upon reading the paper, delivered yesterday, by William Berry and Richard Johns,[1] this House do say; That if the rights and privileges of a free born Englishman, settled on him by Magna Charta, so often confirmed by subsequent parliaments, can be preserved by yea, and nay, in wills and testaments, and other occurrents, the Lower House may do well to prepare such a law, and that the Upper House will consider of it."

Subsequently, the Quakers presented an able and logical argument for a change in the law concerning oaths. It opened with the following dignified and eloquent preamble: "We are Englishmen ourselves, and free born, although in scorn commonly called Quakers, and therefore, so far from desiring the least breach of Magna Charta or of the least privilege belonging to a free-born Englishman, that we had rather suffer many degrees more than we do, if it was possible, than willingly admit of the least violation of those ancient rights and liberties, which are indeed our birth-right and so often confirmed to us, by subsequent Parliaments. And had we not been full well assured that our sufferings may be redressed, and our request granted, without the violating of Magna Charta in the least degree, we would not have desired it."

[1] Richard Johns was a distant relative of the founder of Johns Hopkins University at Baltimore.

The argument had a good effect, and the Lower House of the Assembly voted for a modification of the statute, but Lord Baltimore did not give his approval.

The period was arriving when the cause of the Quakers was to receive a powerful impulse. As William Penn, the son of a British Admiral, in early life a student at Oxford and Paris, heard of the oppression of his fellow religionists, under the statutes of Maryland and Virginia, he conceived the project of "a free colony for all mankind," wherein entire liberty of conscience should be allowed.

From the hour that Penn made his treaty under the shade of the elm trees on the Delaware, Quakerism was more respected.

The men that began to build on the rectangular streets of the newly surveyed city of Philadelphia, were industrious, and glad to welcome as sharers in the municipal government, the Jew or the Turk, the Calvinist or Roman Catholic.

Not long after he sailed up the Delaware he proceeded to visit the societies of Friends on the tributaries of the Chesapeake. Subsequently he made a second visit and conducted Lord and Lady Baltimore[1] to a religious meeting at Tred Haven. Richardson, who was one of the preachers, describes Lady Baltimore, as "a notable, wise, natural, and courteously carriaged woman."

---

[1] Lady Baltimore had been the widow of Henry Sewall of Patuxent, one of the councillors of the Province.

After Penn's return to England, Quakerism was strengthened in America, by the arrival of Thomas Story, another man of cultivated intellect. He had received in England a complete education, and was not only a proficient in Greek and mathematics, but also skilled in the arts of music and fencing. His associations in youth were with an excessive ritualism. The church he attended conformed to the "new fangleism" that crept back again to the Church of England in the days of Archbishop Laud. For a time he was very zealous in the observance of rubrics, but in time they became a burden, and at length he bounded over to that Society of Friends, which well nigh forgot that man was a compound of flesh and spirit, and demanded a few expressive rites.

Having studied law, Story came to Pennsylvania, was made Master of the Rolls and Keeper of the Great Seal, and subsequently Mayor of the city of Philadelphia.[1]

On the 27th of the 3d month, 1699 O. S., he attended the yearly meeting of the Quakers at West River, County, Maryland, in company with a distinguished physician of Philadelphia, whom Penn called, "tender Griffith Owen." On the 13th of the next month Story says in his journal, "came one Henry Hall, a priest of the Church of England, and with others of his motion eaves-dropped the meeting, but came not in." Richard

[1] Story, in 1706, married a daughter of Edward Shippen of Philadelphia.

Johns, a prominent member of the meeting, then arose, and made the following confession of faith.

"We believe that the Lord Jesus Christ, who was born of the Virgin Mary, being conceived by the promise and influence of the Holy Ghost, is the true Messiah or Saviour; that he died upon the cross at Jerusalem, a propitiation and sacrifice for the sins of all mankind; that he rose from the dead on the third day, ascended, and seated on the right hand of the Majesty on high, making intercession for us; and in the fulness of time shall come to judge both the living and the dead, and reward all according to their work."

The next day the clergyman and his friends again lurked near the meeting, and Story says:

"My companion in his testimony apprehending they were within hearing, cried aloud to them to come forth out of their holes, and appear openly like men, and if they had anything to say, after meeting was over, they should be heard."

Story next challenged them to prove their call to the ministry," which they, taking upon them to do, only told us that Christ called the apostles, and they ordained others, and they again others in succession to that time."

Then Story demanded proof "who they were that the apostles ordained, and who from age to age successors ordained, wherein if they justly failed they were to be rejected as no ministers of Christ, since they had rested the matter on such a succession." "Many people," continues the journal, "called out to the clergyman. 'We will pay you the tobacco, being obliged by law, that is forty pounds of tobacco for every negro slave, but we will never hear you more.' While we were yet in the gallery one climbed up into a window, and cried out with a loud voice to Henry Hall, 'Sir, you have broken a canon of the Church; you have baptized several negroes, who being infidels, baptism ought not to have been administered to them.'

"At this the priest was enraged, but made no answer to the charge, only fumed and fretted and threatened the man to trounce him.

"Then I observed to the people that if these negroes were made Christians in this sense, members of Christ, children of God, inheritors of the kingdom of heaven, received into the body of the Church of Christ, as the language is at the time of sprinkling, how could they now detain them longer as slaves? Several justices of the peace being ashamed of their priest, slid out of the meeting as unobservable as might be, and the people in general contemned them as such, who behind the back of the Quakers had greatly reproached and belied them, but face to face were utterly subdued by them. That night several of the justices, lodging with our friend Samuel Chew,[1] expressed their sentiments altogether in our favor, and

[1] Samuel Chew was the son of Samuel Chew of Chewton, Somersetshire, England. He was a physician and became Chief Justice of Delaware. His son Benjamin, was born on West River in 1722, studied law at the Inner Temple, London, and ultimately became the Chief Justice of Pennsylvania.

the priests were really ignorant men in matters of religion."

Sir Thomas Lawrence,[1] the Secretary of the colony, wincing under the plain arguments of Story, complained of what he called the tart expressions of the Quaker, to the Lords of Trade and Plantations. William Penn being in England, his attention was called to the subject, to which he alludes in a letter to a friend:

"A silly knight! Though I hope it comes of officious weakness, the talent of the gentleman, with some malice. Matters there are never attacked by Thomas Story, nor in irreverent tones.

"I never heeded it, only said, that if the gentleman had sense enough for his office, he might have known this tale was no part of it, that Thomas Story was discreet and temperate, and did not exceed in his retorts and returns.

"But 'tis children's play to provoke a combat and then cry out that such a one beats them; that I hoped they were not a committee of conscience and religion, and that it showed the shallowness of the gentleman that played the busybody in it."

At the commencement of the eighteenth century the Quakers exercised a powerful influence in the colonies. Men were forced to admit, that they were keepers at home, industrious, intelligent, not given to

[1] Sir Thomas Lawrence, son of Sir John, B't, having spent all his estate was made Secretary of Maryland in 1696 and in 1712, died there.— *Notes and Queries,* Dec. 27, 1873.

wine or brawling, cleanly in their habits, and honest in their commercial transactions.

The yearly meeting of the Society was eagerly looked for by all classes. Edmundson well observed, "Yearly meeting in Maryland, many people resort to it and transact a deal of trade with one another, so that it is a kind of market or change, where the captains of ships and the planters meet and settle their affairs, and this draws abundance of people." Occurring as it did near the Whitsuntide holidays, the black slaves flocked thither to enjoy rest for a few days from the exhausting labors of the tobacco field. Families from the different counties rolled there, in ponderous old-fashioned carriages for the purpose of social reunion, young men came on fine horses, to compare them and give a trial of their speed, and others went to confer with the beautiful and pure minded maidens, who, in their plain drab dresses and scooped bonnets, were to them far more interesting than the angels, who seemed cold and distant, because they had neither flesh nor blood.

The accession of James the Second to the throne of England, although he was in religious sympathy with Charles Lord Baltimore, brought trouble to the Proprietary of Maryland.

The King, fond of arbitrary power, determined to make all of his colonial governments directly dependent upon the Crown, and in April, 1687, ordered a writ of quo warranto to be issued against the charter of Maryland, but before there could be a hearing of the case, James was an exile, and William and Mary by the revolution of 1688 ascended the throne.

Taking advantage of the new order of affairs in England, John Coode a clergyman, the Titus Oates of Maryland, described as a "democratic Ferguson in principles of government, an Hobbist or worse in principles of religion," became the leader of the party in the Province in favor of abrogating the charter.

In April, 1689, was formed " an association in arms for the defence of the Protestant religion, and for asserting the rights of King William and Queen Mary to the province of Maryland and all the English dominion."

A statement was printed for them, by Richard Nuthead at Saint Mary, a copy of which is preserved in the British Museum library, affording the first evidence of a printing press in Maryland.

After the accession of William and Mary, the King of England appointed the Governors of Maryland. Lionel Copley was in 1691 commissioned as Governor, and soon after his arrival an Act for the establishment of the Protestant religion was passed, and the ten counties divided into twenty parishes.

The opposition of the Quakers was so great that the law was a dead letter. After the death of Copley, in 1694, Nicholson became Governor, and with him, there came in the month of August, six clergymen,[1] making

[1] Dickinson, a Quaker preacher, under date of 8th 11mo, 1695 O. S., writes at the Downs:

" Several priests were going over into Maryland having heard that

the whole number in the Province, nine. He succeeded in passing a law forbidding public worship to Roman Catholics, but in 1695, under the influence of Quakers and Romanists, the invidious legislation was repealed, but the very next year it was enacted, that the Church of England in the Province, should enjoy all the rights, established by law, in the kingdom of England, and it was proposed that a Bishop should be appointed, who should, as a representative of the clergy, have a seat in the Upper House of the Assembly.

The Rev. Dr. Thomas Bray, who had in 1696 been appointed Commissary for the clergy, in company with Sir Thomas Lawrence, Secretary of Maryland, waited on Anne, the Princess of Denmark, to request her acceptance of the respect shown her by naming the capital of Maryland, Annapolis. Bray having received a donation for libraries from the Princess, he presented books to the amount of £400 to the capital. Some of these books are still on the shelves of the library of St. John's College in that city, and on the covers is stamped "De Bibliotheca Annapolitana.[1] In March, 1700, Bray arrived and preached before the legislative Assem-

the Government had laid a tax of forty pounds of tobacco on each inhabitant for the advancement of the priest's wages."

These were probably the clergymen recently ordained at Saint Paul's Cathedral, London.

In 1698 a Rev. Mr. Gaddes was at Annapolis, and Rev. Chs. H'y Hall at Herring Creek.

[1] The following is from the book of St. James Parish: "1698. Books received ye Rev. Ch's H'y Hall —— May. A Catalogue of books belonging to ye library of St. James Parish in Ann Arundel Co., sent by ye Rev. Dr. Bray, and marked thus "belonging to ye library of Herring Creeke, Ann Arundel County."

bly at Annapolis. At this session, it was reenacted, that the Church of England should be the established church of Maryland. As before, the Quakers used their influence with the King, to prevent, while Dr. Bray went back to England to secure, its approval.

The biographer of Bray writes: "Though the law, with much solicitation and struggling, was preserved

The following parochial libraries were sent to Maryland by Dr. Bray in the course of a few years.

		Books
Annapolis,		1095
St. Mary's,		314
Herring Creek,		150
South River,		109
North Sassafras,		42
King and Queen's Parish,		196
Christ Church, Calvert County,		42
All Saints,		49
St. Paul's, Calvert County,		106
Great Choptank, Dorchester County,		76
St. Paul's, Baltimore	"	42
Stepney, Somerset	"	60
Porto Batto, Charles	"	30
St. Peter's, Talbot	"	10
St. Michael's	"	15
All Faith's, Calvert	"	11
Nanjemoy, Charles	"	10
Piscatoway, "	"	10
Broad Neck, Ann Arundel	"	10
St. John's, Baltimore	"	10
St. George's, "	"	10
Kent Island,		10
Dorchester,		10
Snow Hill, Somerset	"	10
South Sassafras,		10
St. Paul's, Kent County,		35
William and Mary, Charles County,		26
Somerset, Somerset	"	20
Coventry, "	"	25
St. Paul's Talbot	"	2

from being totally disannulled, yet many of the exceptions which the Quakers made against it, sticking with the Lords of Trade, all that could be obtained was, that Dr. Bray might, with advice of Council, draw up another bill, according to the instructions of that Board, and sending the bill to Maryland, had the promise, that his Majesty, upon its return, would confirm it."

The law drawn up by Dr. Bray was submitted to an Assembly begun at Annapolis, the 16th day of March, 1701–2, and was approved by the King. It was styled "An Act for the establishment of religious worship in this Province, according to the Church of England: and for the maintenance of ministers."

The Act provided, that "the dissenters, commonly called Quakers" should have the privilege of making a solemn affirmation or declaration instead of the usual oath.

Although absent in body, the interests of the Episcopal church in Maryland were not forgotten by Dr. Bray, and a Rev. Mr. Hewetson, of Ireland, was recommended as superintendent of the clergy. In a letter, written at Chelsea, August 27, 1703, and addressed to Mr. Smithson, Speaker of the Maryland Assembly, he alludes to the rude treatment by the Governor, of himself and the clergyman, whom he had suggested for suffragan or commissary, and proposes that the Maryland legislature shall set apart one of the best parishes, as the cure of a suffragan, to be appointed by the Bishop of London, and build a house for his residence. He further suggests that the glebe should be stocked with ten negroes, twenty cattle, and twenty hogs. It had been proposed, that the suffragan should have a seat at the Council Board of the Province, but this did not receive his approval, and he thought that this officer should not reside on the same side of the Bay as the Governor of the province.

We enter not upon the eighteenth century. The aim of this little book has been attained, if it has brought to light a few facts not hitherto published relative to the mode of life, the struggles, and principles of those who were the founders of Maryland.

ADDENDA.

CLAYBORNE FAMILY AND ARMS.

THIS family from an early period, dwelt in Westmoreland, on the borders of Cumberland.

In the days of Richard the Second, there was a knight of Westmoreland, Robert de Clyborne, who bore on his arms the Saxon motto "Clibbor ne scearn" which has been variously translated, "A burden shames not," "Untouched by shame," or "Adversity no Disgrace."

Over the door of Cleburne Hall erected in 1577, near Westmoreland, not far from Penreth, Cumberland, is cut the same arms given to Robert Clyborne in the Visitation of Cumberland, published by the Harleian Society; quartering of four. First and fourth argents: three cheverons interlaced in base, chief sable: second and third, argent saltier engrailed vert, over all a mullet for difference.

The Visitation of Cumberland calls the father of William Clayborne of Virginia, Edward; and his grandfather Robert, but some writers state that his father's name was Edmund, and his grandfather's Raphe or Rich'd, the result perhaps of careless transcription.

Thomas, an elder brother of the Virginia Clayborn, in 1580, married Agnes daughter of Sir John Lowther, of the distinguished family of Lowther Hall, Westmoreland.

A son of Thomas, named William, resided in Tipperary County, Ireland, and in the ancient church of Kilbarron on the east side of Lough Derg near where it flows into the Shannon, not far from Killaloe, is a stone over a vault, in the chancel with the following coat of arms, and inscription:

Crest.— A Dove and olive branch.

Arms.— Argent three chevronels braced in base sa. A. chief and bordure of the last.

Motto.— Pax et copia.

INSCRIPTION.

Gulielmus Cleburne de Ballicultan, obiit vigesimo secundo die, mensis Octobris, Anno Domini, 1684.

William Clayborne on his return from England, as Treasurer of Virginia, sought for 3000 acres of land, near Potomac Creek, and perhaps it was through his influence, that the Legislature of Virginia, in 1653, designated the region from Machodac Creek to the Falls of the Potomac, Westmoreland County.

SIR EDMUND PLOWDEN.

SIR Edmund Plowden was the great grandson of Edmund Plowden the distinguished jurist whose commentaries on law, Chief Justice Coke called " exquisite and elaborate."

Francis his grandfather born in 1562, married in Oxfordshire, and died in 1652, at the age of ninety.

Edmund resided after his marriage, about A.D., 1610, at Wanstead, Hampshire. His wife, was Mabel, daughter of Peter Mariner of that place.

Although he had been educated a Roman Catholic, before he came to America he conformed to the Church of England.

In 1632, he petitioned King Charles, for a tract of land, to be " exempted from all appeal and subjection to the Governor and Company of Virginia, and with such other additions, privileges and dignities, like as have been heretofore granted to Sir George Calvert K't, late Lord Calvert in New Foundland, together with the usual grants and privileges that other colonies have for governing, and ordering their planters and subordinates, and for supplying of corn, cattle and necessaries from your Majesty's Kingdom of Ireland, with power to take artificers and laborers there."

In June, 1632, the great seal of State was affixed to the charter of Maryland, and issued to Cecil, the Second Lord Baltimore, and the next month Charles the First, from his court at Oatlands, issued an order for a grant of land in answer to the petition of Sir John Lawrence, Baronet, and Sir Edward Plowden Kn't. The king writes:

"Our pleasure is, and we do hereby authorize and require you, upon the receipt of these, our letters, forthwith to cause a grant of the said Isle, called the Isle Plowden, or Long Isle between 39 and 40 degrees North Latitude, and of forty leagues square of the adjoining continent * * * * to be holden of us, as of our crown of Ireland, by the name of New Albion, with such privileges, additions and dignities to Sir Edmund Plowden, his deputies and assigns, as first Governor of the premises, etc."

Plowden appears to have been a choleric and eccentric person. In the year 1635, his wife Mabel complains, to the High Commission Court, that because she refused to sell an estate, which she brought on her marriage, twenty-five years before, worth £3000 per annum, her husband had treated her with extreme cruelty. By the persuasion of friends, the complaint was dropped, and the wife consented to return once more to Plowden's house, but he soon began, as before, ill treatment.

Another complaint on May 3, 1638, was lodged by the Rev. Philip Rofield, for twenty-five years rector of the parish of Lasham, Hampshire, for beating his wife, about to become a mother, because Plowden and the clergyman had disagreed upon the terms of a certain lease.

In the year 1634, Captain Young and his nephew Robert Evelyn commenced the exploration of the Delaware River, and other parts of the province of New Albion. After this voyage Evelyn returned to England and in 1637 received an appointment as Surveyor of the Virginia Colony. In 1641 there was published a small quarto with title "Direction for adventurers, and true description of the healthiest, pleasantest, and richest plantation of New Albion, in North Virginia, in a letter from Mayster Robert Eveline, who lived there many years."

At the time of its publication Plowden was still in England. The first sentence of Evelyn's letter is as follows:

"Sir Edmund, our noble Governor and Lord Earl Palatine, persisting still, in his noble purpose, to go on with his plantation, on Delaware or Charles River, just midway between New England and Virginia, where, with my uncle, Young, I several years resided, hath often informed himself both of me, and Master Stratton, as I perceive by the hands subscribed of Edward Monmouth, Tenis Palee, and as Master Buckham, Master White, and other ship masters and sailors whose hands I know, and it to be true, that there lived and traded with me. And I should very gladly according to his desire have waited upon you in person, had I not next week been passing to Virginia."

In concluding the letter, Evelyn remarks: "If my Lord Palatine will bring with him three hundred men, or more, there is no doubt, but he may grow rich. * * And truly I believe my Lord of Baltimore will be glad of my Lord Palatine's plantation and assistance, and against any enemy or bad neighbor. * * * * I shall entreat you to believe me, as a gentleman and Christian, I write to you nothing but the truth, and hope there, to take opportunity, in due season, to visit you, and do all the good offices in Virginia, my place and friends can serve you in."

In 1642 Plowden was residing in Virginia, and in 1648 by way of Boston he returned to England, where the same year he published a description of the Province of New Albion in which are the following statements:

"After seventeen years discovery there, and trial made, is begun to be planted and stored by the Governor and Company of New Albion, consisting of forty-four lords, baronets, knights, and merchants; who for the true informing of themselves, their friends, adventurers and partners, by residents and traders there, four several years, out of their journal books, namely, Captain Browne, a shipmaster, and Master Strafford his mate; and by Captain Claybourn fourteen years there trading, and Constantine his Indian, there born and bred; and by Master Robert Evelin four years there, yet by eight of their hands subscribed and enrolled do testify this to be the true state of the country and Delaware Bay, or Charles' River."

Allusion has been made to the fact that in this book

a year before the passage of Maryland Act on Religion a scheme of toleration is presented.

The precise date of Plowden's death has not been ascertained but his will was made 29th of July, 1651, in which he styles himself "Sir Edmund Plowden, Lord Earl Palatinate, Governor and Captain General of New Albion in North America."

His sister Elizabeth, married Sir Arthur Lake the son of Sir Thomas who, like Sir George Calvert, was a Secretary of State, under King James and before 1634, she was a widow. The facts in this notice have been obtained from Visitation of Oxfordshire, Description of New Albion, Strafford's Letters, Bruce's Calendars of State Papers and Burke's Landed Gentry.

THOMAS COPLEY, S. J.

THE warrant of protection, given by order of Charles the First, to Father Copley, printed on the ninety-second page of this volume, was obtained upon the plea, that he was tarrying in England, attending to his father's estate.

In the Calendar of State Papers for 1634, under date of 1st of December, Thomas Copley, in a petition to the King, states, that he is an alien born, and therefore conceives he is not liable to trouble, for his religion, by the laws of the realm, yet fearing he may be molested by some messengers, while following occasions which concern his father's, and his own estate, prays his Majesty to refer this petition to one of the principal Secretaries.

The attention of Secretary Windebank was called to the request, and on the 10th of the month, the warrant was issued.

SHIP WARWICK.

HUBBARD in History of New England states that Ferdinando Gorges with John Mason, George Griffith and other associates, employed men for several years, to search for a great lake, in province of Laconia, for which, in 1629, they had received a patent.

The ship Warwick, in the summer of 1630, arrived at Piscataquay, New Hampshire, bringing as passenger Capt. Walter Neale to act as Governor of the infant settlement in that region.

INDEX.

CORRIGENDA.

Page 91, Caption. Bark Virginia, should read Bark *Warwick.*
45, Running title. Takes the oath, should read *refuses* the oath.
66, Richard William, should read Richard *Willand.*
71, Oxoniensis, should read *Oxonienses.*
87, Edward Hawkins, should read Edward *Watkins.*
103, St. Jingo, should read St. *Inigo.*

www.ingramcontent.com/pod-product-compliance
Lightning Source LLC
LaVergne TN
LVHW011223110826
845150LV00006B/1530

* 9 7 8 1 4 2 5 5 1 6 2 2 2 *